Forty

*The Year My Husband
Became a Quadriplegic*

written by
MICHELLE RUETSCHLE

The book you hold in your hands will be a powerful encouragement to you, no matter what trials you face. Their story is that inspiring!

Joni Eareckson Tada

Author, speaker, and founder of Joni and Friends International Disability Center

If this account does not, on occasion, move you to tears and cause you to rejoice at the outcome, you need to check your pulse to insure your emotional batteries are not depleted. I highly recommend it!

Harold J. Sala, Ph.D.

Author, speaker, and founder of Guidelines International

This book is one of the most important gifts I have been given to take in the broken body of Jesus and the holy promise that I, too, will rise and walk again. This labor of love will free your heart to dance in awe and wonder with the goodness of God.

Dan B. Allender, Ph.D.

Professor of Counseling Psychology and Founding President
The Seattle School of Theology and Psychology

In a beautifully crafted, riveting account of a miraculous story, Michelle Ruetschle reminds us all that deserts are a pivotal part of how God forms and refines us. Whether you are deep into a desert, on the precipice of one, or just emerging from one, you will find hope, comfort, and wisdom on every page.

Ron Carucci

Best-selling author of Rising to Power; The Journey of Exceptional Executives *and columnist for* Forbes *and* Harvard Business Review

This book should be read by all who suffer and those who suffer alongside. It is poignant and practical. I found myself tearing up on one page and laughing out loud on the next. What Michelle has put to pen, God used to soak my heart.

Daniel Hahn, D.Min.

Lead Pastor Encounter Church and co-director Catalyst International

Michelle's story is so riveting that it is impossible not to turn the next page. If you loved Romeo and Juliet, you will adore this book. If you like cliffhangers, this will be like none other you have read. If you are going through your own desert experience, then you will have a companion that knows sorrow and yet can guide you with the compass of hard won joy. This beautiful, glorious book will change your life.

Becky Allender

Co-founder of The Allender Center of Trauma and Abuse
The Seattle School of Theology and Psychology

God has given Michelle the capacity to capture deeply ripping human emotions in evocative words and images, through which she took me, in tears, to the Love that never lets go.

Dr. Darrell Johnson

Preacher, author, former pastor of Union Church of Manila,
Teaching Fellow for Regent College, Professor of Preaching for Carey College

Forty: The Year My Husband Became a Quadriplegic is a challenging and powerful story of courage, love and trust. As Michelle shares the journey from heartache and despair to hope and miraculous recovery, I wept and laughed. Both her and Steve's faith in God shines through at all times, inviting all of us to strengthen our own faith no matter what we face in life.

Christine Sine

Author of Sacred Rhythms: Finding a Peaceful Pace in a Hectic World
and co-founder of Mustard Seed Associates

In her book *Forty*, Michelle Ruetschle lets us walk with her as she relives the courageous recovery process of her husband, Steve, following a nearly fatal motorcycle accident. Her determination to keep their relationship one and their love fresh is an example to all of us.

Darlene Sala

Author of Created for a Purpose and Encouraging Words and speaker

This book is a gift. A costly gift. Gently wrapped within the parchment of pain tied together with the tangled threads of grace and hope.

Mandi Els

Author of Mandi's Story *and speaker*

Forty

The Year My Husband Became a Quadriplegic

By Michelle Ruetschle

For Union Church of Manila.
You loved us through our story and you welcomed us back.

We are forever grateful.

CONTENTS

PROLOGUE

It is no accident that the story recorded here is divided into forty reflections. In the Bible, the number forty is often linked to a time of testing or trial. When God flooded the earth during the time of Noah, he caused it to rain for forty days and forty nights. Moses, Elijah and Jesus all fasted for forty days and forty nights during key moments in their ministries where their faith and endurance were tested. Moses sent spies into the promised land for forty days. When they returned, their overall lack of faith caused God to return the entire Israelite nation to the desert, retracing their steps all the way back to the Red Sea. When Jonah went to Nineveh to warn its people of impending judgment, he spent forty days urging them to repent. Jerusalem was destroyed in a mighty judgment forty years after Jesus prophesied its demise with weeping.

No life is lived without trial. This book is about a particular time of trial in my life and in the life of my family, when the force of life's circumstances came down hard upon the foundations of my faith. Reduced to the barest bones of myself by the severity of events unfolding before me, the groundwork of my life was exposed. The strength of my beliefs, the endurance of my love for my spouse, and my trust in a good heavenly Father were all tested by the wide reaches of the calamity that befell us, its effects rippling out over many months and then years.

Even as the specifics of my own story unfolded, I quickly saw that the pain and testing of that time was like a bridge into the painful stories of others. In the telling of my story, others saw elements of their own. I have always been a fan of memoir for this reason. Rather than attempting to outline a generalized approach to faith in times of trial, we as listeners to each other's stories can build our own bridges of connection and understanding. The resulting infrastructure, a web of storytelling, is far more organic and deeply true than any systemic approach because we are forced to find and build it together, doing the hard work of listening, to someone else's story and to our own.

If trial and testing is a major theme in this book, then the desert is its most fitting geography. Steve's accident occurred so unexpectedly and with such ferocious intensity as to require a natural metaphor all its own. When I realized that flash floods can occur in a desert landscape, and can in fact be exceptionally devastating under those circumstances, the metaphorical theme was sealed.

Biblically speaking, deserts are a testing ground from which spiritual transformation can emerge. The Israelites remained in the desert until their spirits had been pruned of a mindset induced by four hundred years of slavery in a foreign land. They emerged one generation later, ready to be radically obedient and actively participate with God in claiming His promises. Elijah, worn out and tempted to despair by an idolatrous Israel and the relentless persecution of Ahab and Jezebel, trekked into the desert to Mount Horeb where he encountered the very presence of the Almighty in a whisper. Jesus, following His baptism and directly preceding His active ministry, was tempted in the desert.

In each case, only an utter reliance on God allowed them to survive. The Israelites relied on the pillar of fire to guide and protect them at night, and manna to feed them. Elijah was fed by an angel and given a holy rest to prepare him for his forty-day trek toward his encounter with God. Jesus countered Satan's temptations with scriptural truths, submitting His own power in faithfulness to His Father.

My journey in the desert required a similar dependence. Deprived of normal comforts and distractions, I was forced to address my essential need of God. In the midst of so much scarcity, His presence was more apparent, a vital companion from which I took both guidance and nourishment. Without Him I may have survived the desert, but I would not have emerged the same: physically and emotionally depleted to be sure, and yet somehow spiritually enriched. This is the tension that you will find in these pages: that while humanly there was struggle, loss and devastation, spiritually there was comfort, renewal, and growth. I do not wish to diminish the former by emphasizing the latter. Both were present in equal measure.

While many biblical truths came alive for me during that time, one particular verse stood out:

> *So we do not lose heart. Though our outer self is wasting away, our inner self is being renewed day by day. For this light momentary affliction is preparing for us an eternal weight of glory beyond all comparison, as we look not to the things that are seen but to the things that are unseen. For the things that are seen are transient, but the things that are unseen are eternal.*
> (2 Corinthians 4:16-18)

No affliction is the same, nor can any real suffering be considered light or momentary except in contrast to an eternal weight of glory. In sharing my experience, I can neither codify nor make understandable what is mysterious and unseen. I can, however, describe the tension between simultaneously wasting away and being renewed. My forty reflections are a dance between these two realities, the human suffering and my hope through faith in Jesus Christ.

This is my desert story, unwound in forty short reflections.

Steve has preached his story from the pulpit and shared it in seminars. Someday I hope that he will write it down. In the meantime, I can only honestly and adequately articulate my own. In the telling, I hope that together we can take heart as we peer through a mirror dimly, looking toward glory.

FORTY

1

THE GROUND GIVES WAY

One week before the accident.

———◆———

God is our refuge and strength, a very present help in trouble.
Therefore we will not fear though the earth gives way, though
the mountains be moved into the heart of the sea.

(Psalm 46:1-2a)

Steve turned forty the year he had his accident. It seemed significant, straddling the mid-point of life on legs still strong, yet with sufficient experience behind him to know the general direction forward. I made him an album full of photographs and notes from family and friends, a varied assembly gathered from across his several careers as artist, musician and pastor, across cities and now continents. Our older boys drew pictures and presented him with gifts found in the garden of our home in the Philippines, dirty rocks and half-crushed flowers offered up like treasures. The youngest of our three, still toddling on uncertain legs, bore only kisses and the gift of his sweet-smelling skin pressed up against Steve's scratchy cheeks, chubby fingers gripping his shirt.

That summer, we visited Steve's parents in Ohio, as part of our yearly trek to the United States from our home and ministry in Manila. We looked forward to these visits every year, reconnecting with dear family and friends, refilling our tanks for another year of ministry. Steve had gone off for an adventure with his younger brother—a motorcycle trip they had planned for months. They had driven south to join a team of motorcyclists and instructors for a three-day training course and tour that would bring them back up north. Today was their first day on the road. I did not mind staying behind with the children, soaking in the quiet of the large house, the hush of soft carpets, the pleasant views of perfectly manicured lawns stretching out like a sea of tranquil green, the relative cool of an American summer.

Steve's mother was watching our three boys, while I attempted to contain the usual debris packed for our long sojourn abroad. Clothes, books, toys—enough for two months' worth of activity—spilled forth from our luggage, the happy refuse of children at play. I was thinking about dinner when the first low note of unrest sounded. I barely noticed the phone's ring, accepting the handset from Steve's mother with casual indifference.

Surprisingly, Steve's older brother, Mark, was on the line. This was unusual, and I found my senses quickening ever so slightly with the unexpected nature of it. Without preamble, he told me that Steve had been in an accident. No, he did not know very much. They were taking Steve to a hospital in Asheville, North Carolina. Perhaps we should go. Should he drive?

The words landed gently at first. Still fooled by the innocuousness of the day, I was not alarmed. Only a flicker of worry passed over my heart. *Oh shoot,* I thought, *poor Steve. He must have broken something. He will have to be laid up all summer. Of course, I will go.* I informed Steve's mother and rushed to throw a few things in a bag. There was no time to let the information penetrate deeply, a vague sense of disquiet easily drowned out by the harmlessness of my surroundings. Nonchalantly, I kissed the children and stepped out, the ground still firm and sure beneath my feet. Sensing my calm, the children easily accepted that I would be seven hours away and waved goodbye.

It was early evening when we departed. Mark drove. I sat next to him in the passenger seat as we glided over smooth freeways, directing us impassively toward our destination. As the day faded gradually into night, my certainty began to wane with the light.

We all know, theoretically, that life is precarious. Earthquakes can demolish the steady ground we take for granted. Deep below the surface the rock is in constant motion, hot and fluid. And yet we persuade ourselves that it is safe enough to set our weight upon. We expect the earth to rise to our feet.

It was Steve's younger brother, Mike, who sounded the first real warning. Talking to him on the phone as we drove, I sensed faint signals of distress rising up from beneath the stated facts. Our conversation was brief, both of us still warily circling the details, failing to ask the difficult questions. Mike was the first to find my husband at the scene of the accident: Steve by the side of the road, conscious but in excruciating pain. The ambulance arrived and took him to a helicopter waiting on a flatter, safer spot along the sharp curves of the Blue Ridge Parkway.

I tried to pin some assurance to Mike's words, but they flowed unpredictably and I could not find my way among them. There was something wrong with Steve's neck. He needed immediate surgery. I heard the words, but my brain could not arrange them into a pattern that made sense. They seemed to stubbornly float above my consciousness, out of reach, afraid to land.

Meanwhile, we were flying into the surrounding darkness toward answers, passing nameless towns, the growing shadows swallowing up the surrounding scenery. As the hours passed and night fell, we could see only a few feet before us, hurtling mile upon mile down unfamiliar roads. My mind was as blank as the view from my window. I remained frozen in the face of the ominous words. Surgery...neck. I had not been able to connect any of the isolated bits of information into a meaningful chain. The phone rang occasionally. I volleyed questions into the oncoming darkness like flares. They fizzled and died. Still, I could not grasp what lay ahead.

The surgeon was the first to strike a match as we continued to speed through the darkness. With each sentence, the faint outlines of our future life began to take shape. He had just finished operating on Steve. I was surprised that he would take the time to talk to me, as yet unaware of the seriousness of the situation. He talked straight, without inflection, drawing clear lines in and around the nebulous details I had failed to grasp. He said it simply: Steve had broken his neck between c6 and c7. There had been significant damage to his spinal cord. Occasionally someone could come back from this but it was rare. A ten percent chance of any meaningful movement below his shoulders.

The surgeon's final words illuminated the future with a terrible flash of light: Steve would most likely never walk again. It hit me full force, then. A seismic shift had occurred. The ground had given way.

This was both an ending and a beginning. I was watching some mysterious collaboration of events violently rend the fabric of my life in two, the past falling away irretrievably while I stood helpless on the other side. Like the Israelites after the parting of the Red Sea, I stood dazed on an unfamiliar shore as mountains of water towered and then crashed upon all that I thought I knew of my life. For them and for me, it would be both a terrible destruction and a deliverance. Through catastrophe, a definitive line had been drawn. There was no turning back.

It was water that separated the Israelites from their former life and propelled them into the desert. Water, an ancient symbol of chaos, crushed their oppressors but also erased their former life. Had they known they would spend forty years in the desert, depending exclusively on the Lord, realigning their minds and souls in the discipline of the wilderness, would they have rejoiced? Like them, I had no idea of the impending journey. I only knew that I had suddenly been dropped into unfamiliar and hostile territory without any supplies or a map.

2

HOW WILL YOU LOVE?

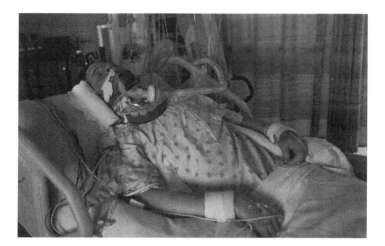

Steve in ICU.

—————◆◆—————

But for right now, until that completeness,
we have three things to do to lead us toward that
consummation: Trust steadily in God, hope unswervingly,
love extravagantly. And the best of the three is love.

(1 Corinthians 13:13, The Message)

It was well after midnight when Mark and I arrived. As the car turned into the parking lot, the hospital glowed with quiet assurance in the darkness. Virtually deserted at that late hour, we made our way among the maze of starkly lit hallways toward a destination still obscured.

It felt as if we were burrowing deep into the building, toward the Neurological ICU, to the place where my husband lay, already post-op. As we stepped from the elevator into darkness, I peered into a waiting room shrouded in gloom. My brother-in-law's tenuous shadow slumped alone among the empty chairs, a smudged comma bracketed by their orderly rows, receding into black.

Immediately, I felt the thing that needed to be said push urgently to my lips. Sure and true, it had sat crouched and ready at the tip of my tongue since I'd heard the news. "It's not your fault." We hugged and wept, Mike's body still stiffly suited in his motorcycle gear.

We perched uncomfortably on the edge of the chairs while Mike relayed more of the facts. No one saw the accident. The bikers were making their way around winding roads, and Steve's mishap occurred perfectly hidden within a sharply curving bend. Mike was the first to find him, rounding a corner to find Steve in shock, frozen on his back in a ditch on the side of the road, his motorbike lying askew nearby. Steve had been certain that he was dying. Unable to move, he looked into Mike's face and said, "Tell Michelle and the boys that I love them. Please take care of them for me." In his anguish he was crying out loud to Jesus, asking Him to save him, heal him, even as he was strapped into a gurney and loaded into the ambulance. Together they rode to where a helicopter was waiting farther up the ridge. Then Steve was taken away, lifted airborne, leaving Mike to make his own slower way to the hospital. Steve had immediately gone into surgery. As Mike remembered and I imagined Steve, alone and afraid, we wept again.

At the same time, another part of me was gathering itself up. Even as we sat talking and crying, this part of me was disposing of the moment, the tears. One thought began to overshadow all others, every detail falling away around the sharp, cutting certainty of it: I had to devote every second to loving Steve. Whether loving him meant letting him go or willing him to live was neither clear nor relevant, only to love.

Catastrophe has a habit of reducing one's life to its barest essentials. Under its intense pressure, few things can stand. In that moment, for me, only one thing remained. There was no time for the romance of it. Rather, there was an almost ruthless quality to the truth thus exposed. Love. Not the soft, sweet, shifting shape of feeling but the driving essence of it, that powerful and resolute force that exists beyond time and place. I knew with momentary clarity that it was the only thing that could bear the weight of this monstrous event. It was the only sure foundation. My feet planted thus, I saw clearly. In my mind, I adjusted the shutter speed and aperture of my thoughts. Turning the lens, the background blurred as my love came into stark relief. I focused in on love.

When I was finally permitted to see Steve, it was 3 a.m. We

exited the dim waiting room into the bright glare of the ICU. Straight ahead and slightly to the left of the nurse's station was his room, curtained behind sliding glass doors. Stepping in, Steve's bed was central, an island of white linen. To the left of the bed, machines functioned with quiet efficiency, reading his oxygen intake, his heart beat, his blood pressure. On his right was the ventilator that kept him breathing. From one or both sides the various IV drips stood like sentinels over the bed. Below, appropriately obscured from vision, were the bags with body waste. In the corner near the window, a lazy boy that would soon become my bed.

Steve laid utterly still among the monitors, whose beeps and clicks measured what little life was left. I was told that the nerves affecting his chest area were traumatized, whether temporarily or permanently we could not know. This, along with the inflammation in his neck from the surgery, was obstructing his breathing. They were keeping him deeply sedated so he wouldn't struggle against the respirator. The nurse compared it to "breathing through a straw."

In spite of Steve's condition, I sensed, impossibly, that his spirit was still present though his body was not. Even as he laid immobile and silent, I knew that he was there and that he wanted to live. The soul opened up, cried out. It did not need a tongue to be heard. They say that newborns die if they are not touched and held. What little life remained in Steve felt like that newborn, tenuous and utterly dependent. He did not respond when I held his hand, yet I sensed that he might like my fingers in his hair. I leaned over the bed, willing my presence to be known.

I sat down and took his hand, threading my arm carefully around the life-sustaining tubes. As I covered his hands with mine, taking in the scene, a veil momentarily parted. A hint of something beyond came near and touched with gentle yet burning clarity. The same essential question came with a different nuance, here beside the still body: how will you love? It is strange how quickly all else is revealed for what it is, an inconsequential, passing matter. There is a breathtaking simplicity to what remains. The body cannot hold it. In that room, in that moment, it lingered at the portal to the other side.

Later, he would tell me that he stayed alive for me. With Jesus on the other side, there was every reason to move on. But I was not wrong. My love really did keep him here.

3

HARD PRESSED

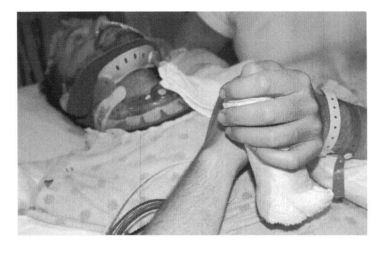

———— ◆ ————

*And being in agony, he prayed more earnestly; and his sweat
became like great drops of blood falling down to the ground.*

(Luke 22:44)

The ICU functioned on a strict and unwavering schedule, a cruel rhythm to which my days now kept time. Visits were limited to fifteen minutes to a half hour, four times a day. Walking away was a brutal act, tearing at the flesh and wrenching the heart. In the beginning, I wept with each departure. It took enormous willpower to put one foot in front of the other leading me away from my beloved, whose life was balanced so precariously among the machines.

During those precious minutes in his room, however, time often slowed. There is a translucence that hangs around the edges when life's grip is loose. The air feels thin. The light is different. As Steve hovered just this side of another realm, I tasted my own ephemeral estate. We waited together quietly, then, suspended in the hush in between.

At other times, there was a physicality and immediacy to our moments together, the violence of Steve's fight for life fully evident. He would come into consciousness and buck up in pain and panic against the ties that bound his arms, and the weak strains of breath coming through the small tube in his throat. In confusion, he barely registered that his arms responded only halfheartedly to his terrified efforts, his fingers bent uselessly into his palms, like gentle fists. Never fully aware, he did not realize that his legs needed no tethers, resting motionless under the sheets. I leaned in and spoke soothingly to him then, running my fingers through his hair, where sensation remained.

In those earliest of days, we were hard pressed. Survival was paramount, without regard for the future and with no understanding beyond each given moment. With a past that was unrelatable and a future that was unknowable, the present grew large, expanding to bridge the distance, a massive territory measured in minutes and hours. Steve mostly drifted and sometimes fought his way across the expanse, barely conscious, while I noticed every small detail, hyper vigilant. Navigating the same space on seemingly separate planes, I looked for any way to connect. Most visits, all I could do was endlessly stroke his hair, where he might still feel my touch, and hope that he knew my presence.

When Jesus was hard pressed, He wept blood in a garden called Gethsemane. It is, in fact, the Hebrew word for an olive press. Steve and I once saw one in Israel, a massive, high stone under which was placed a small handful of olives. Only a tiny rivulet of oil would emerge from underneath that great weight, the essential life of the fruit. In Gethsemane, the weight of Jesus' impending sacrifice induced His life blood to come forth with His tears. Under the weight of my own small suffering, what poured out of me was prayer.

It was not a conscious choice. Rarely were there words attached. My being blindly and instinctively sought its source. Neither hopeful nor desolate, I knew only to submit to something more, a presence in the absence. While many seek answers in their Bibles, I was surprisingly relieved to find that under the circumstances, mine offered none. Rather, prayer and the words I found in Scripture opened a window. I did not need to understand what lay beyond, in this life or the next. Nor did I grasp for assurance. I only pushed the window of my soul wide open, felt the breeze and received the light reflected into the room.

We cannot know whether Jesus prayed many words that night. The gospels record only a few. We do know that His body spoke loud, throwing itself to the ground, sweating blood. Words are sometimes inadequate in prayer. I knew in those early days that they were not required. I did not need to line up my faith along logical lines, building constructs with words. It sufficed to simply be with the devastation and allow my soul to cry out.

4

GRACE

Steve and I on our wedding day, 2000.

———◆———

Let us then with confidence draw near to the throne of grace,
that we may receive mercy and find grace to help in time of need.

(Hebrews 4:16)

Steve and I met in the context of tragedy. One after another, heartache upon heartache rocked our own lives and the lives of our friends. Our community gathered during the summer that we came together in a state of shock and sadness. Amidst all of that raw vulnerability and in the sweetness of fellowship brought on by the shared suffering, we were caught up in an unexpected grace. We fell in love. Deeply aware of the undeserved merit of the happiness we had found, grace became the hallmark of our love.

We came together with a gentle certainty. The connection, once made, was irrefutable. Within days we were discussing marriage. The timing was wrong, however, too soon and in the middle of too much grief, rudely interrupting a much more appropriately somber time with its notes of elation. After much discussion and prayer and inward wrestling, we decided nevertheless to step into what felt like an already existent river, flowing naturally onward. Steve wept away an old life even as he stepped into the new. Having both emerged from relational heartache, we unwrapped the gift in wonder. It turned out to be a blessing in disguise, allowing love to be born into the mess. Grace was a constant touchstone as we entered in, undeserving of this new beginning. We spent it extravagantly on ourselves and on each other. With peace in our hearts, we received the gift. Within five months, grace ringing in our ears, we were married.

Grace became our banner, our theme song, and eventually, our calling. Shortly after getting married, Steve entered the ordination process to become a Presbyterian minister. Six weeks after our wedding date, I discovered we were expecting. After the birth of our son, I left my job as a lawyer to be with my child and support Steve in his vocation. These were profound shifts, and yet we continued to sense a deeper current guiding these new directions, an extension of the river into which we had stepped when we joined our lives together.

In ministry and in life, we encountered again and again the redemptive power of grace. Quite simply, we found that we could not navigate the complexities of marriage, of parenting, and of ministry without it. The longer we walked the path of grace, the more we were required to know our own need of it, and thereby extend it more readily to others. Our call to an international church in the Philippines only caused us to throw ourselves ever more frequently at the foot of Grace itself, as we were pushed far beyond the confines of our own capacity and understanding. As we sought to authentically follow Christ in that new calling, grace was most often not a choice but rather a necessity. Again and again, we found ourselves thirsty and drank from its well, washed clean and renewed by its redemptive flow. Without grace, we would not have made it.

Grace is not an inherent quality or characteristic of the human personality. It is an active, relational dynamic, the hallmark of God's life and love in our spirits lived out. We draw upon heaven's limitless supply; therefore, its potential impact is boundless. Grace covers our limitations with its infinite resources, washing us unceasingly in forgiveness, and binding our defective souls together. In our needful estate, it makes love possible. In the God-drenched trenches, it is grace that

19

engineers redemption out of all of the failure and loss.

To truly surrender to grace, however, is to acknowledge one's profound need of it. The more generously we wish to dispense it, the more deeply we must receive it for ourselves. And in opening our hands to receive the gift, we surrender control, we loosen our grip. No treasure is more worthy yet more painful to acquire. There is a Throne of Grace, but we do not sit upon it.

As it turned out, this familiarity with our need to both receive and dispense grace was priceless preparation for the journey ahead. To boldly approach and receive mercy, again and again, was key to survival in a context where much grace was required. Any pretense toward perfection and wholeness was quickly eradicated when Steve's body was broken so profoundly. Yet again, grace would make love possible.

5

SURRENDER

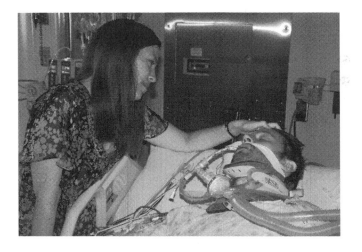

Truly, truly, I say to you, unless a grain of wheat falls
into the earth and dies, it remains alone;
but if it dies, it bears much fruit.

(John 12:24)

In those early days, I often felt like I was drowning. Nothing could have prepared us for the kind of force that came so quickly, destroyed so fully, and just as quickly receded again, leaving the landscape utterly changed. At times I seemed to float, carried along by inexorable circumstances. At other times, I was submerged, fighting for air. Then, just as quickly, the waters began to recede, revealing a desert waste. We walked in an unvaried landscape of daily regimens, accompanied by a foreboding sense that our circumstances were inhospitable to life. Such was our first taste of life in the desert. The desert life meant a life of extremes: one either had too much water or too little. The danger of flash floods loomed with every storm. There was little that grew there and almost nothing that sheltered.

Somehow, I did not fall apart completely. Moments of peace and clarity were randomly interspersed with utter devastation, grief unpredictably rising and falling in waves so powerful that I could only surrender to the tide. In the beginning I awoke and fell asleep awash in tears. I wept through an entire breakfast. I locked myself in the bathroom of our hotel and knelt on the floor, unable to move. I huddled in the bathtub, letting the tears blend with the water. I bathed often, trying unsuccessfully to cleanse with water a deeper sense of wrong, as if like dirt it could be washed away. Our few remaining possessions and even the children were momentarily irrelevant to me in those moments of grief, when I looked about me, bewildered, thirsty and lost. There was nothing recognizable here, no map, no former way of being that would get me through. While I had others to comfort me, I was keenly aware that the ultimate consequences would be mine alone to bear. Until Steve regained consciousness, if he ever did regain consciousness, I was alone. I could not know yet whether anything we had known endured or whether we would have the resources to survive.

And yet there was an inexplicable certainty anchoring this loss. Despite the grief rocking the surface, something deeper held its place. I alternated between the struggle on the surface where I was impassively pitched and tossed by the waves of circumstances and the deeper currents beneath where all was still. Without any control or power over the unfolding of events, I was both shaken and held fast by forces greater than myself. My whole body cupped open in helplessness, I had no choice but to surrender to the depths.

In those rare and precious moments of utter surrender, a mystery took on flesh and wrapped itself around my life. The yielding strangely engendered joy. This joy was far from happiness. Its parameters were wide enough to amply contain my sorrow. A deep, vast well of it softly undulated inside of me. It blanketed my spirit in silence. It calmed the sea, and like the hushed wonder of an aquatic world, where time slows away from the muted, distant realm of air, a new world began to unfold in my spirit. Under the water of surrender, every quiet word, every gently spoken reality of love and grace could be heard more clearly than ever before.

Utterly helpless and surrendered, I spoke with calmness the unthinkable questions into that quiet. *Will he live? Must I let him go into that greater grace?* With equal serenity the response emerged. *He will live.* I knew it deep as the well itself.

6

A RAY OF LIGHT

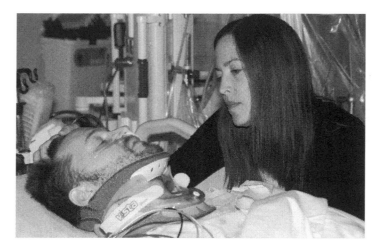

Visiting Steve in ICU.

———— ♦ ————

This is the message we have heard from him and proclaim to you, that God is light, and in him is no darkness at all.

(1 John 1:5)

The waiting room that had once seemed strange and unfamiliar became my home away from home. It soon filled with the familiar faces of family members equally devastated and transported by some randomly tragic event into this unfamiliar world. Like refugees, we banded together in our temporary encampment, with its odd rituals and holding patterns, wondering when we would be permitted to reenter normal life. In the beginning I did not understand the lack of tears, the card playing and the small talk, so incongruent with the gravity of our situations. Later I learned that a soul cannot sustain that intensity of grief day after day without rest.

As if by some silent signal, we all rose a few minutes before the appointed visiting time and filtered past the requisite hand washing stations to the doors of the ICU. There was no rushing, no urgency. We had grown accustomed to the ICU rhythms, understanding what was required, falling in line. We were, after all, utterly at the mercy of this new domain. The proliferation of experts, the unbending rules, and the expensive equipment lent an air of exactitude to the process. Humbled by the greater machine of which we were but a small part, we played our roles accordingly.

As familiarity grew and time moved forward, I became more fluent in the language of Steve's body. Initially, I did not know whether he would return to his former mental state. I was therefore happily surprised by subtle signs that Steve was listening—a small nod yes or no, a lifting of the eyebrows. Though he did not open his eyes, I sensed him responding to my presence, his beautiful spirit engaging with me. Other times I came and went from our visitations without any indication that he knew I had been there. He would moan and shift but could not speak because of the breathing tube. While he appeared peaceful when sedated, he showed increasing agitation and panic when he became conscious. Most times I did not dare to rouse him, knowing that with all of his limited strength, he would use his head and shoulders where movement was still possible to buck against the restraints around his wrists, shaking the prison bars of his dead and heavy limbs. I tried to imagine what it would be like to awaken to the world and find that there was not enough air and the body had flown. No wonder he seemed so lost. Later he would tell me that he had floated into other rooms on the ward, peering in on patients in other beds.

I got to know a woman in the waiting room. Her husband had a stroke while riding his lawnmower. He rolled into the stream behind their house, pinned beneath the machine, half drowned, long before she even noticed his absence. It was hours before he landed here, beneath the clean, white sheets. Each person in the waiting room had a story like that, a story like mine.

We all moved in the rarefied air of that tenuous space between life and death, a sacred interruption of the ordinary. In the gloaming of our normal days, the interplay of light and shade was less obvious. In true darkness, however, the light shone brighter. Steve, like the others, was only partially tethered to the earth. It would take only a small breath of calamity to snuff out what little precious life remained. While I was more clearly bound to the earth, my heart followed his, peering in to the other side. Faith is not a candle. It is a ray of light from a bright and constant sun that pierces the fleeting shadows in which we live. I was straining with him toward its glow, silenced by its greatness. At times, all there was to do was be still in the room and sense its steady rays.

7

THE SAINTS CRY OUT

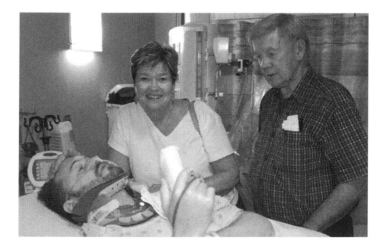

Steve's parents visit ICU.

———◆———

Behold, I am of small account; what shall I answer you?
I lay my hand on my mouth.

...I have uttered what I did not understand,
things too wonderful for me, which I did not know.

(Job 40:4; 42:3)

Trouble always comes. A pastor's wife knows this. At times it brews slowly, a dreaded darkening on the horizon that causes us to pull our coats closer around us and head for shelter, readying ourselves for its onslaught. Other times it strikes quickly, with precision, catching us unaware. However it comes, the water eventually beats down. The storm upon us, we often stand and shake our fists. Preposterously, we attempt to take on the heavens. We rail with thin, small voices at the clouds as if they might listen. We wrestle with the wind as if with our tiny fists we could buffet it into submission. Who do we think we are, equal with the universe, contending with the Almighty? Exhausted, we eventually find our knees. And wait.

This time, I had no warning. I was instantly leveled, immediately on my knees, breathless. I took no time to shake my fists, so great was the force of this particular outburst. And yet I had not quite perceived the severity of the storm already upon us. I was too busy trying to keep dry amidst the myriad troubles of each day to look up and find my bearings. A future reality was gathering itself upon the already threatening horizon, thick with added gloom. No one had uttered the word *quadriplegia*.

Sometimes in the storm, the top priority surfaces like a piece of wood out of deep water. Prayer. True to its nature, it surfaces from the deep of a thousand other pressing needs and floats there, as sure of its place under the sun as the water itself. There is no formula to prayer during these otherworldly days, no expectation. It is simply essential, more important than every visible, concrete need that asserts itself from every side.

I am clear, however, that in this circumstance prayer need not be a solitary function. Grief can easily form an island, a barrier to those who have not walked the same path. When calamity is huge, however, it is not wise to remain in isolation. It was not enough to pray alone. I needed others to join me.

I asked Steve's brother Mike for a journal and he gave me a laptop. Dear friends created a website so that I could say the hard things only once and yet reach many. Each day, I wrote my prayer requests down on the computer and posted them to the site. Each day, there were scores of answers. Each day, the news spread and more and more prayers were lifted up on our behalf. Every church Steve had worked in, every person we had met through our international ministry, Christians and non-Christians alike, spread the word, a vast network that grew with every like and every share. Laying aside all pride and self-sufficiency, I did not hesitate to ask the whole world for prayer. Miraculously, the whole world answered. In over a hundred countries, by the thousands, they prayed with me for Steve. Alone with his inanimate presence, I was far from solitary. We all gathered under a human banner of helplessness. Together the saints cried out. While I knew that I mattered, I also knew with beautiful, painful precision my place. The bent posture of my core, the pressing in, the utter surrender meant that I could not demand, but only ask with open hands, knowing full well that all was "too wonderful for me."

Daily there were prayer points, which I shared on the site. Steve went in and out of fevers and in and out of consciousness. We tried various pain medications, weighing the different side effects. He rarely slept. A second surgery was scheduled that would insert a cage around his spinal cord to hold it in place and allow it to heal. A bad case of pneumonia came and went, delaying surgery. Every day, the prayer points were crucial and life threatening. Every day, the prayers and encouragements flowed in in response.

We had lost an entire way of life, cut away with the same precision and finality as Steve's surgeries themselves. And yet in its absence something new had been given that was just beginning, a pouring in of love, a pulling together in the common ache and shared language of loss. I sensed that as I allowed the pain to be shared and carried collectively, there was an opportunity for all of us to be altered in a deeply painful but beautiful way. Together we could be sifted, together we could look with greater clarity at what mattered. Together we could gather up what good was left and reflect the light.

In our prayers, the universe was set right, with me far from its center. A plumb line had been drawn and all had organized itself around its truth. Even as the prayers went up, a quiet within reflected the words of Job. I laid my hand upon my mouth and was silent.

8

TRUE NORTH

Aidan and Jude's pictures for their Papa.

━━━━━━◆━━━━━━

Unless the Lord builds the house,
those who build it labor in vain.

(Psalm 127:1a)

There was a burden I could not carry. I could not think of my children. I could not bear to add their pain to mine. Aidan was eight at the time of the accident, a deep thinker, serious and kind. Jude, a year younger, was a constant whirlwind of activity, both affectionate and rambunctious. Our youngest, Zephyr, was barely two years old, still soft and chubby with baby fat, too young to understand. In the days following the accident, my thoughts were only of Steve. My singularity of purpose was partly born of necessity but also partly a survival mechanism. If I considered the potential violence done against their tender souls with this grief, I might perish.

The children's response to our sudden predicament defied reason, however. There were only a few tears. According to their grandparents, they slept well at night. I could not explain it. The Lord had taken them and swaddled them in a supernatural sense of security. To this day, they speak of that time with greater hope than sorrow. Somehow, I understood and received the miracle of this provision, and my worry was lifted from me.

The day came when they arrived at my hotel room near the hospital, these precious boys who loved their mama and papa. They were young, their hearts still compasses attuned to our direction. If we were well, then they were well also. Together we sat among the beds as I told them the facts, simple and unadorned. The two older boys listened solemnly, nodding their heads, while Zephyr played around us. We were all calm, even as I told them their papa would most likely be in a wheelchair for the rest of his life. They did not seem to mind this news at all, their faces registering neither shock nor grief. Their most pressing question was both practical and immediate: how long would he be in the hospital? God's grace and a child's wisdom. They knew intuitively that the truest thing they could receive from their father had little to do with his body. It was his love and presence they longed for, and they would have it, still.

We all have an inner compass, except that as adults we choose the direction in which we will walk. As Christians we are called to assume the posture of a child and sync our compass with our Father. With childlike receptivity, we attune ourselves to His orientation. If He is well, then we are well also. And He is always well. This is why the apostle Paul can sing in his prison cell, or why a bereft man can declare that it is well with his soul. A child does this intuitively with his parent. For us it is a gift received through the Holy Spirit, the sense that no matter what is happening in our circumstances, all is deeply, truly, eternally well in Christ.

This is a mystery, that one can be both deeply sad and profoundly well. To be soulfully well is not to be without sadness. Rather, the sadness resides within a greater wellness in the same way that time rests inside eternity. When a child falls, it hurts and they cry. Scooped up into a parent's arms, their wound still hurts and yet a greater comfort shifts the narrative. The tears may continue and even increase or they may hush, but regardless of the state of their anguish, the trust of the child and the love of the parent draws a circle around the pain.

Immediately after sharing with them every detail I could

think of regarding our new situation, I had the big boys draw pictures for their dad. Their images were incredibly insightful, despite the freshness of the facts upon which they relied. In Jude's picture, his dad was in a wheelchair, smiling, imagining his family as it was when he could walk, with Zephyr perched upon his shoulders, all of us standing, happy. In Aidan's picture, Steve was sick in bed, attended by a nurse and dreaming of his accident, a motorbike spilled across the road and he lying in a ditch. In childish hand Aidan had written, "Dear Papa, I am sorry you brock (sic) your neck. I hope you feel better."

They drew matter-of-factly and handed their pictures over happily, these heartbreaking images of our new life. After that, we played together with the gifts others had thoughtfully provided. Though the house had crumbled, their foundation had not moved. Their compasses pointed in my direction, and I was also surprisingly calm. In the midst of the wreckage, they looked not at the fallen walls around them but into my face, and knew that all was well. I, in turn, tuned my inner heart to His. I too chose not to determine my wellbeing by the surrounding rubble. I set my direction true north. I set it on my Abba, Father. And like my children, I knew from His face, that while the circumstances were not good, it was well with my soul, and therefore all was truly, deeply, profoundly well.

9

RETURNING

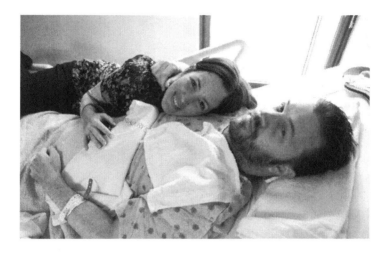

Now faith is the assurance of things hoped for,

the conviction of things not seen.

(Hebrews 11:1)

Hope for healing was difficult to navigate. I hovered between a tenuous faith in complete healing and a desire to submit to whatever God's will might be for Steve's life. At times I felt hope arising in me, even as I also prepared for the worst, with a hundred possibilities in between. I was uncertain about what faithfulness required of me. Did it require an unwavering confidence in a happy, near-impossible ending? Did it require submission to a difficult path? In Scripture, many of those commended for their faith are first given a specific word or a promise in which to put their trust. Noah, Abraham, Moses, Joseph, and so many others were given clear instruction. The words they received were neither elusive nor obscure. In many cases, the word was accompanied by a sign or an angel or a vision in order to fortify the recipient for the inevitable persistence required to follow. There seemed to be little uncertainty as to the command itself. Rather, receiving the promise required both a willingness to believe the impossible and an obedience to accept what was required.

I envied those faithful saints the clarity of the command received, but I could not envy them the road of faith that followed. Scripture says that, "(s)ome faced jeers and flogging, while still others were put in prison. They were stoned; they were sawed in two; they were put to death by the sword. They went about in sheepskins and goatskins, destitute, persecuted and mistreated—and the world was not worthy of them. They wandered in deserts and mountains, and in caves and in holes in the ground" (Hebrews 11:36-38).

Not knowing any more than that my beloved would survive, I waited in a posture of attentiveness, assessing my willingness to believe for the impossible while also bending my spirit to accept what might be required. I was watchful, listening intently through what I heard and saw. While it was agonizingly slow and replete with setbacks, I began to see hints of progress. Steve had survived his second surgery and his breathing tube had been successfully removed, allowing him to breathe on his own. While he remained heavily sedated by pain medications, we had found a method of sedation that was more calming, and his arms no longer needed to be restrained. Where before he was still and fighting silently, now Steve began to vocalize and move those parts of his upper body where the nerve connection remained intact. When he moved his arms weakly and awkwardly, I thought: he will feed himself! When his fingers curled slightly, I thought: his fingers will come back, he will be able to type, and one day he will hold my hand again! When he moaned, I thought: his vocal cords are intact, he will speak! And so faith arose in increments along with the smallest of signs.

The trick was not to run too far ahead. Thus far, I had received no great word, no clear promise, no obvious sign. Did I believe that my God could do a miraculous healing? Indeed, I did. Did I know that God sometimes permitted suffering and even death for His beloved children? I did. Was I clear that much was required of the faithful saint in the fulfillment of God's promises? Yes. Faith was a dance; it required partnership with the living God, responding to His lead, willing to trust His choreography, straining together in the more difficult moves. I would hope for what He led me to hope for, I would listen for His next instruction, and I would lay down what was needed in order to follow.

Until then the signs of hope had been so slight, tenuous evidence of what might come. Because Steve floated in and out of consciousness, I sometimes wondered whether he even knew my presence. Much of what I hoped for was entirely uncertain. I was therefore astonished when a nurse came in one day to ask him a few questions and check his mental status. She asked him where he was and he said, "North Carolina." She asked him what kind of building he was in, and he said, "hospital." Finally, she asked him who was sitting next to him (me), and without missing a beat, the patient who had barely said a word all week spoke out with clarity and confidence, "my wife... the most beautiful woman in the world."

I wept with joy. He was here, he was returning.

10

FLIGHT

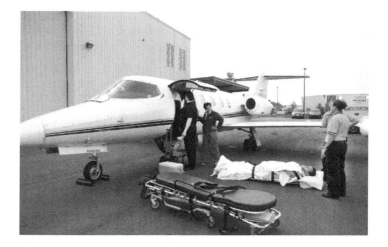

Getting ready to load Steve onto the jet.

———◆———

The Lord is close to the brokenhearted
and saves those who are crushed in spirit.

(Psalm 34:18)

Two weeks after the accident, we passed beyond the threshold of merely keeping Steve alive. He was finally lucid, beginning to acknowledge his accident though not quite ready to explore its consequences. In this regard, he spoke most often of his deep anguish over causing his loved ones so much suffering. He would let this thought fall into words and then move quickly on to some other topic, as if by touching on it lightly he might lessen the blow. He preferred to speak on lighter subjects, talking about the children, thanking and praising his nurses, showering me with love and compliments, and generally exuding the particular brand of light and kindness and humor that had always been so naturally his. I was hardly able to take it in—this true conversation, his love eyes present, and his entire spirit filling the room. At the time, it did not seem strange to speak with optimism. The past and the future remained distant, not yet integrated into our understanding. In the vastness of the present, we were simply happy that he was alive.

Despite these moments of brightly colored connection, my love's body was still profoundly broken. While his arms were able to make tiny, weak movements, the rest of Steve's body was immobile. Even his fingers hung limp and inert, as if in despair. He was entirely helpless, unable to sit up, roll over, feed or clothe himself or perform the most basic of bodily functions. Pain was a continuous bedfellow, writing itself in furrows across Steve's brow and making thought and speech difficult.

The future began to assert itself with the question of rehab. A social worker came in to coach us through the process and the paperwork. With great difficulty, we chose to undergo rehabilitation in Seattle, where we had lived for many years, and where Steve had served in several churches. This was a painful decision, as our families would not be there with their invaluable love and support to get us through. Seattle housed one of the best rehab facilities in the country, however, as well as our faith community of many years. We knew that aside from the medical expertise available, we would need to deeply rely on the wide network of our family of faith on the road ahead.

Because Steve's medical condition was far too fragile for public transportation, we flew to Seattle in our own private jet. While it sounded so extravagant when we made the arrangements, in fact, the plane was ancient and tiny. They could barely fit the gurney carrying Steve's motionless body into the cramped quarters of the plane. The nurses had to literally crawl into the few remaining seats. There was no aisle. I was the last to squeeze in next to Steve, propping his arm up on my computer bag so that it did not dangle over the side of his narrow bed.

I discovered to my dismay that the nurses had been misinformed about Steve's necessary pain medications. Somehow I would have to get him through this five-hour flight without them. I prayed quietly and sought the Lord on what to do. The noise from the jet engines precluded talking, so I took out a small iPod and put one earbud into Steve's ear and the other into mine, playing praise song after praise song through the uneventful hours. The flight turned unexpectedly sweet, as I stroked Steve's head and looked out at the scenery below, praises ringing in my ears. It was a quiet miracle. Steve remained abnormally calm and serene despite hours without pain medication. We had found unforeseen shelter in the gentle rhythms of worship.

I watched as the patchwork farmlands of the Midwest shifted into wilder terrain as we glided westward, finally navigating over the snowcapped mountains of the Pacific Northwest. My soul sang as we touched down in this familiar place. I craned my neck out of the window of the plane to catch a glimpse of Mount Rainier's majestic countenance and the beloved fir trees of my former home, then swung my gaze back to Steve, finding him still calmly listening to the music. An ambulance waited for us on the tarmac, carrying us swiftly through familiar streets. There was a joyous sense of homecoming. Until now, we had walked through this fire in a location utterly alien to us, among strangers. Here, we were known.

Reaching the hospital, my sense of familiarity quickly evaporated, however. Harborview Medical Center was the main trauma center for four states. A public hospital located in the highly urban downtown area of Seattle, its ER was lined with every possible form of human suffering, from the tragically injured to the chronically addicted and homeless. Passing through a metal detector to get into the hospital, I knew that I was no longer sheltered from the world, but in it, over my head. While the hospital sat prominently overlooking a city I knew and loved, it's fortress-like walls contained a new culture unlike the one we had known before. I would need to learn afresh.

Doctors and nurses were soon parading through our room, examining Steve with an almost casual sense of routine. In Asheville, Steve had been the only spinal cord injury in the ICU. Here, we blended into an entire floor of patients with similarly tragic tales. As I processed the overwhelming amounts of information, each new and unfamiliar detail bore a disproportionate weight. I felt desperate because I did not know where the cafeteria was. I wanted to cry because I was overwhelmed by the unfamiliar stairs and hallways. I was myopically obsessed and devastated by irrelevant details. I found myself bizarrely longing for the familiar corridors of the hospital in Asheville.

A cloud settled over me as a frantic thought began to dawn: no one was talking about Steve getting better. Just as we had moved from an ICU to a rehab floor, the vocabulary had also shifted, moving from the emergent to the clinical, from the temporary to the permanent. With a shock, I saw what had been there all along. *This would not change. Steve would not improve.* Underneath all of the medical terms, this was the underlying assumption of everything that was being said. So preoccupied with survival, we had not thought to look up at the far horizon until now. The view was wretched. From the heights of the flight we had all too quickly sunk low. I did not yet have words for the darkness that now pressed in, seeming to overpower every fragile hope. There was no choice but to press on.

11

THE GIFT OF HOPE

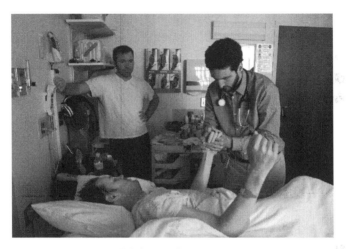

Steve's rehab doctor performs an examination.

---•◆•---

Through him we have also obtained access by faith into this grace in which we stand, and we rejoice in hope of the glory of God. More than that, we rejoice in our sufferings, knowing that suffering produces endurance, and endurance produces character, and character produces hope, and hope does not put us to shame, because God's love has been poured into our hearts through the Holy Spirit who has been given to us.

(Romans 5:2-5)

Strange hope, that knew that God was good when all was wrecked and wretched. Strange to find that something bright remained, untarnished amidst the smoldering embers of a life. Catastrophe had taken what seemed permanent in our lives and demolished it into smoke and ashes that merely floated away, unmasked as the impermanent thing that it was. Grasping the empty air, I found it strangely solid. Something lived where nothing was left.

Hope is a gift. In its purest form, it cannot be conjured up by selfish desire, nor is it deserved. I cannot say why it chose me, only that it did. In His mercy, God drew near, bending toward the desolation, and hope was an expression of His presence. Still, it required something of me. Beyond hope there hovered the threat of disappointment. To trust what flickered so tenderly amidst the embers, and to even fan the flame, was to risk an extinguishing so black that I might not recover.

But for me, it seemed a question of obedience. Hope and faith were linked, and to abandon one was to abandon the other. Sweet grace, then, that hope's notes played with such peculiar certainty into my spirit, lulling me into an unusual trust. Not mine, and yet it came from deep within. I felt beckoned forward, called to confide in the music. It was only a tremulous faith, a fragile note of hope that played both tentative and defiant before the doctors' grim pronouncements.

Steve had shown only the slightest progress in the two weeks since the accident. He was barely stabilized medically, in constant agony and still heavily sedated with pain medication. He could breathe on his own, but only in shallow breaths and with an inability to cough or pull the air deeper into his chest. He could move his arms slightly, but not his fingers. Nothing moved below his chest, though he seemed to have some slight sensation in his feet, which meant that some small communication might still be passing from the lower part of his spinal cord, past the injury, and onward to the brain. Day after day, he simply laid immobile in his hospital bed, reliant upon his nurses and myself for every possible need.

It was an almost playful impulse, then, a vibrant note that bubbled up. In front of the doctor, I asked Steve to wiggle a toe. We all watched in varied portraits of silence as his face contorted with concentration and effort. The movement was barely discernible: one toe shifted slightly. We all leaned closer, unsure of what we had just seen. Try as he might, Steve could not repeat it. But then there was another toe and another. Three toes. A barely distinguishable signal, so small we could easily have missed it had we not been paying close attention.

How quickly perception shifts. Just weeks ago, who would have imagined so much glory in so little a matter? Now a barely visible tremor of life caused hope to leap and bound across the room and rekindle its flame in our hearts. Movement, however slight, in Steve's foot showed that some signal, however small, could travel from his brain down toward the end of his spinal cord. A pure note of joy sounded in that hospital room, a strong pulse of anticipation to briefly shake off grief.

The doctor smiled and upgraded Steve's prognosis. The

tiny tremors in Steve's toes caused the road to curve ever so slightly, shifting direction. We still could not be certain of its trajectory, but something bright glistened among the ashes.

12

BEGINNING AGAIN

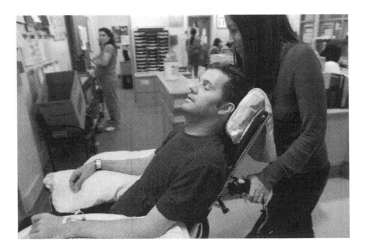

Wheeling Steve through the hospital corridors at Harborview.

———◆———

Then he said to me, "Prophesy over these bones, and say to them, O dry bones, hear the word of the Lord. Thus says the Lord God to these bones: Behold, I will cause breath to enter you, and you shall live. And I will lay sinews upon you, and will cause flesh to come upon you, and cover you with skin, and put breath in you, and you shall live, and you shall know that I am the Lord."

(Ezekiel 37:4-6)

The monolithic fortress of Harborview Hospital seemed unknowable at first, but gradually I began to step out into the ubiquitous hallways, my familiarity growing in ever larger concentric circles as I ventured farther and farther from the safe confines of our room. My first conquest was the rehabilitation floor. The hallways outside our room were glaringly lit by neon bulbs glancing off walls painted an ill-conceived shiny pinkish hue. The family room was poorly furnished with an old couch and a cheap table and chairs. In a tiny kitchenette near the nurse's desk there were large supplies of yoghurt, cheese, milk and ice cream, a promising destination for future visits with our children. Steve's room was a nondescript, gray rectangle, half the size of our room in the ICU. Its saving grace was a beautiful view of Seattle's downtown, the Puget Sound sparkling at its edge, its placid waters stretching toward the snow-capped peaks of the Olympic mountains. Aside from a hospital- issue bed, table, and closet, there was a large recliner in the corner of the room by the window. It folded out into what was almost a bed. This became my outpost, my place of reprieve, my corner residence. Like a bird to a nest, I created my roost there, feathering it with books, binders, get well cards and assorted gadgets. A week into our stay I discovered the gym in a far corner of our hospital wing, a room peppered with strange equipment operated by determined looking therapists and struggling patients. It was difficult to imagine Steve's currently immobile body completing any of the complex contortions I witnessed there.

Throughout our first week, the therapists introduced themselves, and a crowded schedule took shape on a board across from Steve's bed. He could not move, but he would be busy. Every two hours, two nurses came and brusquely hoisted his body into a new position, rearranging an elaborate set of pillows to keep it in place. This process proceeded relentlessly, twenty-four hours a day. On our first morning, a nurse introduced us to Steve's bowel program. It was a wretched and humbling process that took at least two hours to complete. Steve stridently swore that he would never allow me to do it. Neither of us could have predicted then that in the end, we would not be able to bear the thought of anyone *but* me doing it.

This was not a life, but we were living it. Despite ourselves, we grew accustomed to the routine, to the place. Even without a body, Steve was very much alive. Even breathing was difficult, and yet he breathed. Somehow, despite the inhospitable terrain, love grew. There was no rain, no fertile soil, but something was being added, nevertheless. Even as Steve's body wasted away, quite literally before our eyes, his muscles withering with lack of use, spiritually we were being fortified and blown awake.

One day a kind nurse shifted Steve's body to one side in the bed, leaving a narrow corridor along its edge, allowing me to climb in beside him. He could not roll or shift or press into me, but I could mold myself to his still form. I missed his body but it was what lay behind his eyes that I craved most. We looked long and drank deep. It was delicious, our first opportunity for closeness of any kind since his return to consciousness. The usual stream of nurses and therapists continued to drift in and out around us but we did not care. For a few precious moments, we soaked in a precious intimacy stolen from the highly structured hours. All that mattered was here in this hospital bed, and we were both grinning.

It was a beginning. We were rebuilding not just a life, but a marriage: a love that was intended to abide, for better or for worse. We drank awkwardly at first but found ourselves surprisingly full. God was breathing life into our dry bones. It was slow going. Sinews are not knit together overnight and even babies take nine months to fully form. But in this bed we took deep breaths and tasted the promise.

13

ICON

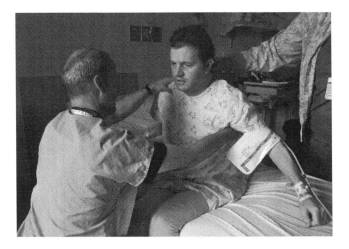

Steve sits up for the first time at Harborview.

———◆———

And lo, I am with thee always, even until the end of the age.

(Matthew 28:20a)

A friend taped a picture of Jesus to the ceiling up above Steve's bed. An icon in classic somber hues, it greeted him each morning as he opened his eyes. Unable to move, Steve would stare at it for long periods of time. He said it comforted him to know that Jesus had suffered on the cross. Pain, he said, was a worthy adversary. Jesus knew it, too.

The first week in rehab, they sat Steve up for the first time. This, like everything, took careful preparation and monitoring. The nurses wrapped his entire legs in nude-colored bandages like a pair of old-fashioned tights, to help keep his blood pressure up. An equally old-fashioned looking girdle was tightly banded around his stomach for the same purpose. These were on top of the pressure stockings that were matter-of-factly wrestled on each morning by strong, adept nurses. Pressure stockings were so tight and difficult to maneuver that loved ones needed to be trained to get them on, a technique that I perfected over the weeks that followed.

It took two people to get Steve into a sitting position at the side of the bed. His six-foot body was dead weight, legs heavy pendulums, arms weak props. He furrowed his brow in pain as he came up, his body straining to simply maintain the position with the help of two aides. As they would do every time he sat up, they connected him to a blood pressure cuff to make sure his heart was able to adequately pump his blood throughout his body. This first time, the machine showed the blood pooling despite Steve being trussed up like a turkey. He became dizzy and miserable within minutes and had to lie down. It was difficult not to be discouraged by the monumental energy required for even the smallest task. Even with assistance, Steve could do nothing for himself.

Our first task was to get him sitting for short periods of time. From the bed he was soon moved to a wheelchair for these exercises. It took two nurses and a medieval looking contraption called a Hoyer lift to do it. It cradled Steve like a large baby in a sling and swung him from bed to chair. Positioning him and letting him down carefully was tricky. One day I would be expected to do all this on my own.

It took a great deal of coaxing to keep Steve from giving up after mere minutes. Gravity's pull on his neck felt unbearable. We had to distract him continually, making conversation, rubbing his arms and head, watching the clock. The first time we reached thirty minutes, there was wild celebration. You'd think we'd finished a marathon. In the narrow world we now inhabited, Steve upright was just as amazing.

Shortly thereafter, we took him outside for the first time in weeks. The breeze wafted through his greasy hair (we had not yet learned the laborious shower chair routine), and he smiled under the sun's warmth. We hungrily drank up yet another tiny freedom given, a handful of minutes on a hospital pavilion tasting the air. Being so thirsty, this was delicious.

How many of these small delights had we missed in our previous life? How many more would we miss again when all this was once more taken for granted? Would we know Jesus' presence in the same way when our lives were no longer confined to a single room; when an icon was no longer the first thing we saw?

I had long known that God does not force Himself into our lives. Nor does He often intervene in our suffering in the ways that we want. Like a child enduring a shot, we want only one thing: we want the pain to stop. But suffering is inevitable. Sometimes there are miracles, but often there are none. Only one thing is promised us in the moment: that He will be with us. Again and again, throughout my life, I had chosen to believe it. He did not bowl me over with the evidence, but He left signs. My life was strewn with these many intimately crafted details, loving tokens of a Constant Presence. It was this intimacy that continued to astound me, the depth of the whispers, the perfectly orchestrated coincidences and, occasionally, the marvelously unaccountable provisions.

When I laid in the small crevice between Steve's body and the railing of the hospital bed, we both looked up into the icon's somber gaze. It stared steadily out from beneath the artist's strokes, neither smiling with an air of frivolity nor theatrically grimacing with pain. The gaze was fixed, holding all the world. It seemed to quietly acknowledge what was, both in that moment and for all eternity. I understood better then the unyielding expression. It did not change. Whatever our circumstance, He remained. Both pain and joy, He knew. All the world and all of time, He held. This sacred truth did not depend on us. From starburst and mountain top He inclined Himself in our direction. He would read the map of our souls and pour Himself into those small spaces. He would lay down His life inside of time, to change everything forever. And in the midst of all that holiness, He would look into our eyes and simply be with us.

14

AT HIS MERCY

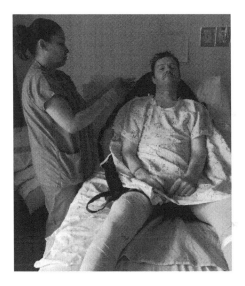

———— ♦ ————

Is not life more than food, and the body more than clothing?
Look at the birds of the air; they neither sow nor reap nor
gather into barns, and yet your Heavenly Father feeds them.
Are you not of more value than they?

(Matthew 6:25-26)

We shared five homes in nine years of marriage, skipping from one to the other like a stone across the water, never stopping. Friends were now packing up our most recent home in the Philippines, storing everything we owned in this world in the church basement. The future was unclear, and so, like ourselves, our possessions were thoroughly dismantled, awaiting some uncertain outcome, sitting in boxes in the dark.

Steve's shoes no longer fit and his clothes were no longer suitable. Nothing was permitted to constrict his body for fear that he might develop pressure sores, which could be life threatening. Soon he would be too skinny for any of it anyway. So I was giving it all away. Even his wedding ring no longer fit the swollen knobs of his fingers. For years, we had held on to our house in Seattle, but its rooms were impossibly tiny and would not accommodate a wheelchair. This too had to go. Mentally I released the furniture, the clothes, the house, and all that tethered us to what we thought we knew. We had no job, no source of income, no home, no possessions. With all of these earthly devices gone, we lost every fixed bearing on the future. Like explorers without navigational instruments or maps, we would have to plot our course with a celestial guide. We were the proverbial birds of the air; we knew that it was He, the source of our very lives and breath, who would have to provide for us now.

Naturally, I thought of Job. Job was permitted to lose far more than I had, but it came with the same electrifying swiftness and finality, a quick and brutal stripping. Yet in James 5:11, I read, "Behold, we consider those blessed who remain steadfast. You have heard of the steadfastness of Job, and you have seen the purpose of the Lord, how the Lord is compassionate and merciful." I searched the story for some sign of that tender mercy and found it in one small line, toward the end of the book, "And God blessed the latter days of Job more than the beginning" (Job 42:12). I pictured Job, surrounded once more by wife and children and ample provision, even more extravagantly blessed than he had been. I could not understand the loss, but the blessing was nevertheless also there, a few sentences almost casually thrown in at the end of the book, a reality that Job lived out over many ensuing years. The words resonated in my soul with personal relevance. I sensed even now God's richest plans and blessings for our future. Although that blessing would probably not come in the way that I hoped, in my best moments, I believed that I would see it.

I am not a lover of happy endings. When I encounter them in books and films, they seem contrived and inauthentic. I prefer the messy process, the struggle in between the beginning and the end. I embrace uncertain conclusions. A story seems more nuanced and true to life when it ends with a question or a possibility. In Job we find no answers, no conveniently simple explanation for the horror of his experience. Instead we are given God Himself. This was enough to silence Job and most of the time, it silenced me as well. No doubt the steadfastness cultivated in Job was too costly to allow the later blessing to be a mere neat and tidy bow on the end of such a disturbing tale. An encounter with the greatness of God silenced Job before the blessing ever came. As they say in Narnia, speaking of Aslan, the Jesus figure, "He is not a tame lion." And yet there was that little line toward the end of Job, that delicious spoonful, adding just enough compassion and mercy to shift the flavor, enough to taste the hope.

We were at His mercy. It was a good place to be.

15

ETERNITY

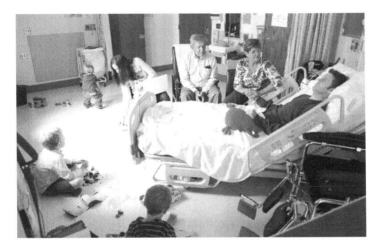

Life in a hospital room.

———◆———

In my Father's house, there are many rooms.
If it were not so, would I have told you
that I go to prepare a place for you?

(John 14:2)

The spinal cord is a mystery. The consistency of toothpaste, it cannot be seen with modern technology. The neat bundle of nerves we imagine flowing from the brain into every part of the body like so many telephone wires is in fact a much more mysterious substance in the spine. How much is damaged, and how it heals is not clearly understood. When the spinal cord is completely severed, however, its victims do not recover. The surgeon's report described Steve's injury as "near complete." The prognosis was bad.

It was a bittersweet day when Steve was outfitted with an electric wheelchair. The chair was both a doorway to greater freedom and an unwelcome symbol of our new life. There was an undercurrent of defeat in mastering such an iconic implement of quadriplegia. As Steve experimented with the chair, we marveled at the sophisticated technology which nimbly responded to the smallest of movements. Though Steve's hands were frozen into claws and his arms were weak, his dexterity with the joystick was remarkable. Overnight I watched him taste independence once more, grinning as he raced through the hallways of the hospital. It was a beautiful sight.

Steve's simple joy at his newfound autonomy provoked a surprising element of melancholy in me. How quickly things had changed. Within weeks of the accident, we had already so embraced our "new normal" that we were almost pathetically grateful for the smallest good thing. While the gratitude was real and beautiful, it also underscored the breathtaking distance we'd traveled in so short a time away from the kind of life others took for granted. We had not yet had time to grieve the enormity of our loss, that beautifully set table of life's richest foods: walking, running, painting, playing the guitar, wrestling with our boys, sex. Not to mention the simpler joys of standing, feeding oneself a spoonful of food, enjoying the feel of a hot shower (Steve could no longer feel hot or cold in most of his body), or giving a bear hug. Instead, we were ecstatic about the crumbs beneath the table. I felt both rich and poor at the same time, a complex interplay of loss and gain.

The severity of our loss forced a new perspective. The eternal context, previously rarely discussed, had moved from its peripheral orbit in our lives to a more central location. The acute revelation of life's unpredictability and the very real deprivation of life's joys provoked a deeper longing for our eternal home. I was peering like a child through a keyhole into that vast room beyond, hushed by the greatness of what I could not understand. From my tiny, obscured vantage point, I felt dizzy with the depths of an infinite goodness in which Steve and I might someday take part. That limitless wholeness of everything made right stood out in stark relief against our brokenness, and even as we groaned with the reality of the present, we longed more deeply for that eternal weight of glory. While we continued to have faith for a more immediate healing, any joy we hoped to find in this trial was rooted more firmly in the eternal promise, not in the assurance of present comfort. As never before, we clung to that future hope.

Long ago I had laid down the question of suffering at the altar of a God who is good, whose foundation is love, and who sees far more than I can see. When I had grappled with the problem of pain, I had eventually arrived at a crossroads where profoundly different conclusions could be made. I chose to entrust my questions to a God who would suffer and die for me. I opened up my hands and gave my questions back to love itself. Fundamentally, it was not for me to understand. Rather, it was a relationship to trust. Now flames had come to test my trust. Somehow, neither Steve nor I were beset by the question "why." We were, in fact, so surrounded by God's presence daily that there was little doubt that He was with us in this valley. That presence of love obliterated the why. Glory seeped through the cracks in our understanding, and by grace, trust stood firm.

Because there was both love and trust, our hearts were open to whatever goodness remained. As we acquainted ourselves with our new normal, we began to notice small evidences of growth in the otherwise barren landscape. Coming upon them, we had a choice: we could either trample these minute offerings underfoot, or we could kneel to admire the nascent promise in every leafy shoot. Humbled as we were, it was not hard to slow down and take note. We knelt to count every sprout and bud, marveling at the grace that allowed such delicate life to subsist where so little water was present. Our marriage was strangely blossoming in the arid soil. Pruned of all that was extraneous to its core, it was already showing evidence of health. One by one, other small flowers bloomed. We heard our children's laughter along the corridors of the hospital. Friends surrounded the bed, massaging Steve's stiffened hands and feet. Our dwindling insurance was met by the generosity of many, often strangers. Astounding acts of kindness were a daily occurrence. Each blessing was a miracle of life.

This is the mystery, the paradoxical mark of suffering in the life of a Christian: the love of God keeps our hearts open to the miracle. We are softened by our trust. Joy thrusts itself up in that verdant soil of faith. Eternity draws near in these small joys.

16

CALLED TO HOPE

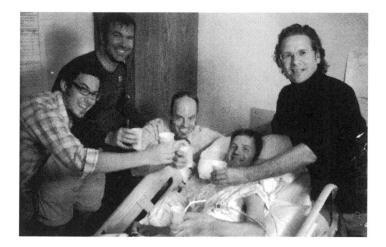

Celebrating Steve's first Pele kick with friends and family.

———————— ◆ ————————

Now hope that is seen is not hope,
For who hopes for what he sees?
But if we hope for what we do not see,
We wait for it with patience.

(Romans 8:24)

Pain continued to plague Steve's recovery. A constant companion, it dictated how long he could bear to sit up to eat a meal; how much attention he could give to a conversation; and most importantly, how much he could work on exercising and moving his body in order to regain strength and mobility.

The hospital sent us a psychologist to show him mental tools to manage the pain. She also addressed the emotional process of healing. Not only Steve's body needed healing, of course; his heart and mind and soul would also need restoration. A licensed counselor, Steve was uniquely able to know and express his inner life. It would be years, however, before words would even begin to be applied to this experience. Like scaffolding on a building, they would be erected according to spare and basic necessity, for the repairs as they took place. This was a deep and foundational work, and progress was slow. Where understanding was insufficient, faith would have to fill in the gaps. I had a feeling that as long as we lived, the work would never be finished.

But Steve was healing. Defying all expectations, he had begun to move his left pointer finger and right thumb ever so slightly. Next he moved his big toe, and one day his entire foot twitched. Nerves began to fire in one small muscle after another in a growing cascade of wonder. None of this was meant to be possible. On this particular hospital floor, the language of hope did not grow naturally. And yet God had planted this seed, fulfilling that softly whispered note of assurance I had felt in my heart a lifetime ago, in the ICU in North Carolina.

He would finish it.

The World Cup soccer tournament had been playing throughout Steve's confinement, a welcome distraction from the long days of therapy and the endless administrative details involved in the rearrangement of our lives. One day, a physical therapist bent Steve's leg and gently prodded his knee to wake up the nerves and muscles. Steve's face strained with effort, as his foot came up to loud cheering in the room. The loudest vuvuzelas at the World Cup could not match the enthusiasm and joy present as we celebrated this little movement. At night a few friends gathered, sneaking in champagne. Steve demonstrated the miracle again, and we all laughed with delight, toasting the victory. We called it the Pele kick.

Miraculous as it was, the healing was also excruciatingly slow. Two Pele kicks a day, and Steve was exhausted. For all intents and purposes, he remained a bona fide quadriplegic. He could not roll over or sit up. We were thrilled that with a simple contraption attached to his hand, he had begun to feed himself. He needed the assistive device to eat because his fingers could not even grip a fork or a spoon.

One of the first things the occupational therapist taught Steve was how to dress himself. The pants were the most difficult. Steve's legs were dead weight, his awkward arms had little strength, and his hands could neither grasp nor pull. I could only stand there and observe as he tried unsuccessfully to manipulate his uncooperative extremities—a grown man in a diaper, fishing awkwardly with stiff arms and limp hands for the prize. He would make several painful attempts before his arms "caught" his skinny leg, all of the muscle gone. Then he would try to heave it up. With all his might he would strain, but he could not do it. The therapist had to finish for him.

On our own, Steve and I spent half an hour trying without success to put on a pair of pants. It was a rare moment of privacy, and Steve wept briefly on my shoulder with frustration and grief. When he stopped himself quickly, I encouraged him to continue, but he said, "Someone will inevitably come in." Someone did come in, a minute or two later. That was the unremitting flow, the unceasing rhythm of the hospital, which gave little room to process grief.

This was our context. Somehow hope would have to take root in this hardened soil. Steve, like so many others before him, would leave this hospital in a chair. He still wouldn't be able to sit up or even roll over without assistance. While everyone prayed for healing, it was difficult to distinguish the human desire from the God-given hope. One is sweetly offered but empty of any spiritual fruit, an utterly human desire to avoid or, better yet, eradicate pain and suffering at all costs. While God does not spurn this legitimate desire, aching with us and gathering each tear, His work is deeper and longer and wider in its scope. His is a holy calling, a faith journey whose essence is submission and whose foundation is trust, for His glory alone. We would have to hold our hope lightly as we followed.

Somehow, I was clear that a fast and miraculous healing would not bring God the same kind of glory a slow healing would. If He wanted my heart, my faith, my hope to root itself deeply in Him, He would have to take it slow. We would have to wait with patience and open ourselves to the work. Only hope would allow us to do that. So every day I opened my hand to hope. I felt called to it in a way I could not explain. Opening myself to both trust and hope was neither logical nor "normal" in this situation, and yet it was God's invitation to me. Knowing that the outcome might not align itself with my desires, I was risking everything to follow. And yet not to hope was a small death of its own, of faith and of future.

So I chose it carefully and tentatively, knowing that indeed God could do exceedingly more than we could ask for or imagine, but also knowing that His glory might shine forth even more powerfully in our brokenness.

17

BE NEAR

Our first date in a wheelchair.

———— ◆ ————

He sent from on high, he took me;
he drew me out of many waters.

(2 Samuel 22:17)

Every night I tucked in the children and then drove back to the hospital. Dividing my time between children and husband, paperwork and phone calls, home and hospital, these stolen moments in the car were often the only times I was alone. What I thought was overwhelming before became exponentially more so now that our children were with us again. It was not the additional time that they required that made it so difficult to balance, but my desire to love and shelter them through this trial, and my inability at times to do so. Every time one of them cried because I was not coming home from the hospital, or because I was sending them off with someone else, I was deeply torn. I longed to be with my boys every minute and I longed to be with Steve every minute and I could not do both. Steve and I missed each other now as much as we missed the kids. Such was the life lived in between worlds, between people, between places, between trauma and hope.

Inevitably, it was dark by the time I made my way back to my love. I was drawn almost unconsciously through the dark to his side. Like a homing pigeon, my instincts guided me back from any distance. If I was late, I had to walk through the metal detectors and endure the suspicious questions of the guards. Sometimes a visitor was still there, but often Steve was alone in the dark room, waiting.

We talked, but mostly we just needed our bodies to occupy the same space. The nights were too long for him without me. They were too long for me without him. For a special treat, I sometimes slept at the house with the children so that they could wake with me. I did not sleep well on those nights. I slept better in the awkward hospital chair in his room, my corner nest near to my love. Steve woke often throughout the night, waiting patiently for the nurses to come to shift his body. Some nurses were better than others, coming in quietly and shifting him gently and efficiently in the night. Others made their presence known, stepping heavily, talking loudly, roughly manipulating his weighty limbs. He was at their mercy for every small thing. We rigged up a bag of water with a tube near his lips, so that he no longer needed to call for help to take a sip. Each night, I took a sleeping pill and barely stirred with each interruption. I rested deeply because I was where I belonged.

Over the years, faith, too, looks like this. One becomes acquainted with the inexorable tide of love, which overwhelms at times in great waves, but then also recedes leaving gratitude in its wake. When the tide is low, one knows it will rise again, as sure as the sun itself. There is a warmth and familiarity that cloaks, providing shelter and rest. Unlike human love, there is a power and mystery that punctuates these gentler rhythms with awe and wonder. Truth pierces and transforms. But fundamentally, faith ushers in a Presence constant beyond space and time. More and more, I just want to be with Him. The more I take in this love, the less I try to deserve it. I just want Him to be near.

18

INTIMACY

JUL 80

Steve's first coffee, during our first date outside the hospital walls.

———◆———

*One of the Pharisees asked him to eat with him, and went into
the Pharisees' house and took his place at the table. And behold, a
woman of the city, who was a sinner, when she learned that he was
reclining at the table in the Pharisee's house, brought an alabaster
flask of ointment, and standing behind him at his feet, weeping, she
began to wet his feet with her tears and wiped them with the hair of
her head and kissed his feet and anointed them with ointment.*

(Luke 7:36-38)

Marriage is a reflection of God and the church. Our identities, Steve's and mine, had been so intertwined that I referred to every aspect of this experience in the plural, ours together. Was God really entwined with us in this same way? What else could justify the sacrifice of one's child but this deep entanglement of one's welfare and experience with that of the other? The Son dies and the Father dies along with him. The children draw near and the Father gathers them up like pieces of Himself. My heart barely had room to carry my three children alongside the heartache. It was full to bursting. And yet He carries us all. What heart is so large as to willingly weave the joys and sorrows of millions into His own?

As with faith, intimacy in a marriage goes through phases. Married only nine years, we had not yet weathered many difficulties. It had always been easy to crawl into each other's most private places. Steve was tender and safe, almost reverent. We had shared ourselves liberally, with joy.

Now it had been two months since we had experienced any kind of privacy. For two months, our intimacy had spilled over into the public sphere. In front of strangers, the supervising nurses, the doctors and the therapists, Steve was required to let me in further than we had ever known. We discussed deeply personal concerns with therapists. I washed him with nurses. We wrestled with his limitations at the gym. And we exchanged both sorrow and love in the constant presence of others. I treaded carefully, aware that this was holy ground. His weakness was exposed, the doors flung wide to places no other person should be permitted to enter. Steve's atrophied muscles and his few awkward motions made him like a new bird, gaunt and ungainly, falling about the nest. While his arms and legs had become thinly cloaked bones, gravity had acted upon his weak chest muscles, forcing them to drop and pool into a soft pouch around his stomach. This was my man, the one who used to delight in lifting me up for a kiss.

He needed me to find him beautiful, still, as he sat naked and helpless in the shower chair constructed specifically for these cleaning exercises, stick-like appendages radiating awkwardly from his soft core. He reminded me of an insect specimen, lifelike yet unmoving, pinned to a board, on display. He was utterly at my mercy, naked emotionally and spiritually as well as physically.

This entrance into deeper intimacy was costly. It had cost us the joy of touch, the loss of carnal knowledge, the playful affection of lovers. The old ways had died, an entire world of pleasure and rapport buried. In its place something new had to arise. We could not yet conceive it. We could only seed the future with this moment, this surrender, this vulnerability, this service.

During our courtship before we were married, we had washed each other's feet. There was no dirt or grime of any substance to wash away, but we took joy in enacting our heart's posture one to the other: in the kneeling, in the mutual submission, in the offering up of our less beautiful parts. A liturgy practiced for centuries, we sought out its origin through its imitation in the present. The living God knelt before those who would betray Him and washed their feet. We knew what it was to be washed clean. We had been transformed by the Savior's kneeling.

At the time we could not have guessed at the evolution of our actions into the current moment. But we knew that this kind of cleansing, this kind of bowing down, would take place in many forms throughout our union, mirroring God's original and perpetual cleansing of us. We knew the grounding of love in sacrifice, as we both offered up our shameful parts to each other and before the tender, forgiving presence of God. It was our best gift to each other: the true marriage vow.

The mystery was this: that the bending and the cleansing felt more like life than death. While something real had died, we were closer to the truth now, to the essence of love and marriage. This latest incarnation came closer to the original act. There was real human refuse to wash away, both on Steve's body and in my own pain and weakness, and the floor came up hard against my knees. I had often been washed throughout my Christian life, offering up my dirty parts, knowing the tender kneeling of my Savior, knowing His healing touch. Now I felt more deeply the meaningful truth behind the act, and the life that came from it. I both gave it and received it. I was the sinner who washed my Savior's feet with her tears and dried them with her hair. And nothing was more precious or true than my gratitude. For she who has been forgiven much, loves much.

19

HOME

SEP 80

Steve with Zephyr on the street near our new home.

————————◆◆————————

Come to me, all who labor and are heavy laden,
and I will give you rest.

(Matthew 11:28)

At the hospital, it took two nurses to turn Steve every two hours in the night. The day nurse administered the lengthy bowel program and gave him his daily blood thinning shot. When Steve needed to be moved into his wheelchair or shower chair, another staff member was called in to assist the nurse. Others taught Steve how to put on clothes or feed himself. Two physical therapists helped manage his exercises and therapy. A speech therapist worked on his lung capacity and ability to swallow. A doctor checked in regularly to monitor his vital signs and medicines.

In six to eight weeks all of these professionals would melt away, and it would be up to me to put on Steve's pants, to administer shots, to operate the unwieldy contraption that moved him from bed to chair, to shift him in the night, and to help remove the stool from his sleepy bowels. Steve was not the only person being assessed in this environment. I too was being trained and instructed in the complexities of his care. When the doctors met as a group to discuss the date of our dismissal from their rehabilitation program, they spoke of whether we were both sufficiently equipped to be released into the world.

In preparation, I had sold our house, signing away our former life in the hospital before we had even begun to step into our new one. God had mercifully provided us with a beautiful temporary place of refuge outside the city. It was all on one floor, with a bathroom and a kitchen that could accommodate a wheelchair. Tragically, our landlord's son had also broken his neck, just three years prior, forcing her to make her home wheelchair accessible. I signed a one-year lease. It seemed a long, bold line to cast into the future, given that we had no idea what was next.

The boys and I moved in to this, our latest set of walls, roof. We created a home out of the new furniture and toys donated by kind friends. Like refugees, we had only a few things by which to remember our old life. I still commuted to the hospital at night to rest with Steve. My corner space next to his bed was most like home to me. The idea of bringing him to the house was terrifying. Neither one of us was ready to leave the shelter of the hospital, the multitude of caregivers, the swarming ecosystem that existed to care for him. But there was no choice. Our Philippine insurance policy was ending, and our medical team was ready to send us off. All too soon we would be on our own.

Sixty-nine days had passed since the accident. It was time to bring Steve home for a test run overnight. We would be on our own for twenty-four hours. He rolled up the ramp of a wheelchair-accessible van donated by a caring stranger and maneuvered his chair into the space next to the driver's seat. I carefully attached four straps from the floor of the car to the chair and put on his seatbelt, just as the therapists had taught me. We might not be able to quickly pop in and out of the car but we were nevertheless mobile. Alone with him in the world for the first time, we took off. I was shaky with both excitement and anxiety.

When we pulled up to the house, our children were waiting. Steve wheeled around, and the kids hitched rides in his lap. We were all trying this on—another home, another body to inhabit, another journey for our souls to make.

For thirty-six hours I ran myself ragged between Steve and the kids. Steve agonized over every request he made, knowing I was already over-extended. He laid helpless in one room waiting for a moment to catch my attention while I dealt with a child in another. Small practicalities began to dawn on the both of us. Not only could I not leave the children, particularly our two-year-old, Zephyr, safely at home with Steve, but I could not leave Steve safely with the children. Our hearts jumped out of our chests when Zephyr climbed into Steve's empty chair, somehow managing to turn it on and nearly pin Steve, who was in bed, to the mattress.

Nighttime proved the most challenging. We both dreaded the alarm, set for every two hours, when I had to get up to turn Steve, rearrange the numerous pillows propping up his body at comfortable angles, and switch the boots that kept his feet from "dropping." I would just begin to drift off again after one of these athletic episodes when Steve had to reawaken me to move a leg or help him in some other way. He felt terrible, and I felt terrible that he felt terrible.

The professionals told us that moving Steve home permanently was going to be hard no matter when we did it. As we waited for state support and funding to be arranged, we were cobbling together an interim plan, feeling around in the dark for what our basic necessities might be, what kind of support the children would be comfortable with, and how in the world I would find time to sleep during the day to recover from the demanding nights. It all seemed impossible.

With all of the moves, all of the anxiety of the ICU, all of the administrative nightmares related to insurance and selling our home and finding a school for our children and every other possible stressor on our lives, it was this moment that pushed me closest to the brink of despair. The immediacy of survival was now gone, the medical support system was about to go away and our community would not be able to drop everything to help us forever. I felt lonely and small and uncertain.

Home is not a roof, it's a family. Whether we liked it or not, all we had was each other. Despite the stress of that first time at home, there had been laughter too. We had young children, and they brought a lightness to the weight of the moment. Steve had to find ways to play with them in his chair. The simple and immediate tasks of feeding and clothing everyone kept me from even thinking about falling apart. And for the first time in sixty-nine days, Steve and I slept side by side in a bed in a room without strangers. Blood is a primitive bond, inextricably linking us together despite the stressors that might otherwise tear us apart. During that time of incredible stress and transition, the very fact of our togetherness and all that it required was a shelter. Whether we liked it or not, we would always be a family.

In my faith journey, I had often strived to be liked by God, working too hard to please Him, at times foregoing my truest self for what seemed more spiritually worthy. I had not always trusted the blood bond. Nevertheless, we too are family, the living God and I. Adoption has mixed my blood with His, and we are now forever bound by the immutable kind of love that resides more in fact than emotion, the spiritual equivalent of a blood line. I had nothing left with which to please Him and no energy to make myself likable. But He was still there, even more there than before, my family, my home. This new understanding was yet another tender shoot to stop and appreciate during this barren season. I went in to my Father and laid down to rest.

20

WALK WITH ME

———— ◆ ————

Fear not, for I have redeemed you;
I have called you by name, you are mine.
When you pass through the waters, I will be with you;
and through the rivers, they shall not overwhelm you.

(Isaiah 43:1-3a)

Ten weeks after Steve's accident, we went home for good. We were like newly hatched fledglings being nudged from the nest too soon, with no feathers and no ability to fly. Somehow, we had to survive on our own. No matter, we would never be ready. Like having a baby, there was no real preparation for this other than doing it.

This was the most nervous I had been. Steve's sister and brother-in-law flew in to help, as did a dear friend. Normally reluctant to receive, I did not say no. The children were excited, and together we drew a poster in bright colors with the message, "welcome home, papa," written in childish hand. My friend found a piñata and hung it in a tree. Together we created an atmosphere of celebration, despite my misgivings.

At the hospital, the staff came around to say goodbye. We had been fortunate; our physical therapists and occupational therapists and speech therapists and doctors had all been excellent, and we were nothing but grateful for their help. A few might even remain friends. Several of the nurses had been Filipinos, a sweet reminder of our home for the past five years. They crouched by Steve's chair for a picture. Everyone was smiling. But we were leaving them now. Most were not even on shift or around during our last hours. They were already moving on to the next crop of patients. We picked up our story along with our things and carried it with us out the door.

All day, I tried to swallow down my overwhelm, large and insistent in my throat. The details were endless. That tiny hump in the rug between the bedroom and the bathroom made it nearly impossible to push the shower chair over. The doorway to the bedroom was so narrow Steve would have to maneuver with careful precision to get through. We cleared out the bookshelves along the wall and filled them with the paraphernalia of quadriplegia: diapers, pads, wipes, rubber gloves, syringes, individually designed contraptions that helped Steve eat and write and grab things, and pills, endless bottles of pills.

Within days, our family and friends had departed, and we were alone for the first time in the desert. Even deserts are prone to flooding. When a sudden storm comes, the desert soil may absorb it poorly. It lacks the infrastructure to cope. Picking up debris along the way, the excess water can be exceptionally dangerous. Flash floods are sudden and can quickly overtake an otherwise dry and sparse landscape. This was a new form of survival. I was alternately dry and thirsty or up to my neck in water. The first weeks, I was ducking debris and trying to swim. The endless demands pushed at me like sudden flash currents. I was overwhelmed, but somehow I was still breathing. I was desperate with love. It kept my legs pumping, treading water. I treaded through the endless nights, through the busy mornings, through the bowel program and the shots and the medications and the endless doctors' appointments, through the children's first day of school. But I knew I could not sustain the pace. I needed help.

The accident had taught us not only surrender, but dependence. We had to rely on others now. I could not take care of Steve and the children at the same time. His morning routine and theirs were equal demands with no room to maneuver. We rolled up the mat of broken sleep to face a day where there were not enough hands. Steve's, with their negligible strength and dexterity, hardly counted.

Reluctantly, we arranged for a service to provide caregivers during the mornings. It took three hours to get Steve ready each day. My two-year-old was a thirsty cup that was never filled. I could not bear to put him away. So when the doorbell rang, I gathered up my courage and let a stranger in.

The man was rough and the woman had trouble learning what to do. Neither of them seemed to have any meaningful experience with quadriplegics. I tried to act normal as I helped these complete strangers handle my husband's lifeless limbs and remove his clothing. I escorted them into our bedroom and into the shower, allowing them access to our most private spheres. I left my lover there, naked and helpless because my child also needed me. The choices were stark when there were just two capable hands and so much need. The caregivers took no joy in their work. I wondered how much the agency paid them and what their lives were like, but they revealed almost nothing. We were an opportunity for them to earn a paycheck, nothing more.

In the midst of this latest crisis, I found the words from Isaiah. God was promising me He would not leave me as I faced this deluge. I hastily tucked this promise into my mind's back pocket. I had no time to meditate on its significance. But weeks later, miraculously, we had found a kind and loving caregiver and developed a rhythm. The children loved him and he cared about what he was doing, much of which was humble work. He served Steve with compassion and found a place in our family. We had found help.

Often, God works quietly. His rescue is not spectacular. He is with you, but still the water comes. He is with you, but still you must swim. The miracle comes gently. Somehow, you have not been carried away by the current. And when the waters recede, He is still there. When the caregiver came, when the routine began to settle, I looked behind and saw a path carved into the desert floor by the water. The flood had carried me somewhere new.

For the moment, I was no longer treading water. I sat in the sand and found His presence beside me. I knew that I needed to keep my heart open to this small miracle. If I could cease to strive for a moment, perhaps I would find a different kind of strength. Perhaps I would come upon God's rescue in a new way. Perhaps I would find myself carried to a new place. There is a strange grace and acceptance that permeates the moments when we are not measuring our progress in human terms, when we are not trying so hard. Then, each time the small miracle comes, our souls know it more clearly: fear not. Rejoice. I am with you.

21

WORKING THE MIRACLE

Steve's first time to stand at the kitchen sink.

———— ◆ ————

Let him bury his face in the dust—there may yet be hope.

(Lamentations 3:29)

September came. The house we rented sat on a secluded lot, surrounded by trees. Every room had windows that looked out on green. Steve and I joked that we would never again have a home as nice as this. It was another of the many extravagant blessings that confounded any simplistic impulse to paint this season black.

The kitchen was the best room in the house. There were windows on every side and a fireplace in the center, by the table where we ate and gathered. A small step or narrow doorway was all it took to keep Steve and his wheelchair out of most homes in Seattle, so our friends came to see us there. Even with the warmth of summer still lingering, I would put logs in the fireplace and enjoy the beauty of the flames. As I cooked or cleaned, I looked out over the verdant splendor of trees and wildlife, a stone's throw from my door. God lives in His creative splendor and I was surrounded by Him. This temporary haven was a safe and gorgeous refuge, a sanatorium for a family limping across days.

It was in this beautiful space that a physical therapist visited us and in a single moment shifted our entire sense of what was possible. Steve could not even sit up on his own, and yet, once she had propped him up into a sitting position on the edge of the bed, she asked if he thought he could stand. We both looked at her and wondered if we'd heard correctly, but a second later, she had pulled him up and he was hanging onto her shoulders, his body tense with concentration and effort. For months I had looked down on my husband, always lying or seated, but now I joyfully looked up to flash him my delight. He was too intent on what he was doing to smile back. What may have been only a matter of seconds, or perhaps a minute, ended, and he was sitting back down on the bed, exhausted and elated. In a flash, we had skipped over countless reasonable milestones and entered an entirely different realm of possibility. It was mind blowing.

The therapist left us with an assignment. Every day, Steve was to wheel himself up to the kitchen sink for his exercise. With a person standing on either side, we were to give one mighty shove, and Steve was to stand up. In front of him was a timer. Gripping the lip of the counter, he would stare intensely out of the window as he willed his muscles to cooperate for the allotted amount of time. At first we set the timer for five minutes, then ten. Gradually we stopped hovering over him in case he fell.

Progress came slowly as we stuck to the rigid disciplines that were required to maintain our lives at this basic level. Each night after the kids were tucked in, Steve and I went through the same routine: the transfer to bed, the removal of his shoes, the heaving of the wheelchair into the corner, the undoing of the belly binder, the checking of the skin for pressure sores, the removal of one kind of pressure stocking and the putting on of another, the undressing which took both of us, the careful arrangement of pillows, the sleeping pills to be gotten and the table placed just so with its morning pill at the ready, Steve's phone within reach in case of emergency, the water pouch hanging with its tube carefully laid within reach, and a sentry of urinals for overnight. We were engaged in a carefully choreographed routine, framed by both care and incapacity. To be sure, there were pinpoints of glory in these daily regimens, but as Steve's brother Mark put it during a visit, there was so much slogging for a few moments of glory.

But little freedoms from these constraints came steadily, as the routine bent and shifted with Steve's ever changing skill set. He could eventually transfer himself to bed for the most part, though he still needed help with small, seemingly inconsequential things, like adjustments to the pillow under his head, or flattening the bedding underneath him so that no wrinkles cause undue pressure to his skin. We experimented with freedom from the belly binder, and someday those impossible pressure stockings would follow. For us, there was a mercifully fluid evolution to our regimen. For others with similar injuries, it remained the same for the rest of their lives.

Sometimes a desert journey might involve a strenuous mining process through rocky obstructions. We were hammering at progress, chipping our way through a tunnel to the other side. At times we came to a point where the rock no longer yielded. Our progress halted, we would feel around blindly for a more promising direction and keep hammering. We toiled and strained in the dark. People often used the word "miracle." They were right. But sometimes miracles are stained with sweat and tears. I remembered the blind man in the gospel of John. Jesus spat on the ground and covered the man's eyes with the mud. It had often puzzled me, the dirt and spit. But now I saw that sometimes miracles are not clean. We were wrestling with the healing on the ground. In the end we were standing, but we were also sullied, covered in the juices of our effort. At night we would fall asleep, spent.

22

REJOICE ALWAYS

Afternoon "stroll" with the boys.

───────◆───────

Rejoice in the Lord always; again I will say, rejoice.

(Philippians 4:4)

The wheelchair had its advantages. Another quadriplegic laughingly told us that he often had to remind his wife that he was not a "horizontal surface." Steve, however, loved being helpful in this way; so when we went shopping or there were heavy loads to carry, we piled them into his lap and walked freely, hands swinging, shoulders light. He reveled in his usefulness and our freedom. The big boys liked to hang onto the back of the chair and hitch a ride. When I tired or needed a cuddle, I curled into the chair on Steve's lap. This way, he still got to drive.

When we were given the gift of a little red wagon for the kids, Steve had the brilliant idea to attach it to his electric wheelchair. This way, he could pull the children along behind him. We found some thick, blue twine and a metal hinge and crafted an attachment between the wagon and the chair. Little Zephyr was the first to try it. Steve maneuvered slowly at first, carefully circling the driveway, but soon they were careening down the street, with me running after them, laughing and breathless. I could not keep up with their blur of motion, but I could hear Zephyr's squeals of delight echoing down the street.

This quickly became our favorite mode of transportation. On cold days we threw in a blanket and snuggled in. Sometimes I joined the tangle of little bodies and we overflowed the wagon's plastic borders, enjoying the wind and whimsy of the moment. People paused to smile at our little juggernaut of family, flesh and fun as we wheeled past.

Living in those moments there was real joy. No heart is capable of absorbing continuous, unbroken sadness, and mine found many things to delight in, even then. The children exhibited even greater resilience, showing no signs of grief at all. Their Papa was there, and they laughed and wrestled and played around his chair just as they used to play around his person. They were neither preoccupied with the past nor worried about the future. Loss lived in the context of what we had before. When we lay down our history, we simply *are* now. My children taught me that the present moment is a great arbiter of grief.

Shortly before the accident, when Steve was still whole, God had given me a verse, an anthem for our holiday in the States. Even after Steve went flying through the air and landed broken in a ditch, I knew intuitively that the verses still held true. Now they swam up from the pages of the letter to the Philippians, worn and familiar. "Rejoice in the Lord always, again I say rejoice." Their exhortation looked different now, and yet the words lived, in the little red wagon and other real delights. Over time, joy spilled over into the loss and mingled there, an ebb and flow of laughter and love and genuine gratitude, all the more sweet because sadness and loss also washed up on those same shores.

The verses in Philippians end with the injunction to think on what is good. What was good was our family still together. What was good was the wind in my face, and my husband's arms around me as we sped down the sidewalk in his chair. What was good was the deluge of kindness we received daily. The list was remarkably long, when I took the time to tally up the goodness. This was no cheap and flowery cover-up, no plastic smile plastered over our heartache. This was simply life as we had come to know it. We discovered that joy is no stranger to the dark.

When Steve was in the ICU, our darkest hour, my brother flew in for a visit. A doctor, he provided priceless perspective and advice. The first time he left Steve after our precious fifteen-minute visitation, he sobbed uncontrollably, hunched down and leaning into the sink, tears dripping into the basin in the corridor where we washed our hands. But later, running an errand with me at the store, I did some stupid, familiar thing and suddenly we could not stop laughing. We laughed and laughed, until our bellies ached. It felt so good.

Joy and sorrow seem strange bedfellows until one experiences moments like those. Having been pushed out into the waves by circumstance, living life with all I was worth, I found that joy and sorrow are part of the same big ocean. Where the swells are large, one extreme flows into the other more quickly and with greater force. In the storm, I was liberally splashed by both.

The verse seems to urge us to always rejoice, but that is not what it says. It says to rejoice *in the Lord* always. His presence is always joy, just as Steve's presence was always a joy to me and my children, whether he was walking or whether he was sitting in a wheelchair. Whether I was cradling my son, laughing and careening behind my husband in a little red wagon, or weeping with my brother over a hospital sink, a Great Presence framed that ocean of human experience. He does not change. Sometimes, the joy He embodies is so quiet and sure, I almost forget it is there. Years of familiarity can breed forgetfulness. Grief, anger, frustration may drift by. Yet joy remains.

23

TRANSFORMED BY GRACE

Happy to be together.

---

*And we all, who with unveiled faces contemplate
the Lord's glory, are being transformed into his image
with ever-increasing glory, which comes from the Lord,
who is the Spirit.*

(2 Corinthians 3:18)

Shortly after Steve and I began our rides in the little red wagon, we also began our visits to the pool. Each development was a step toward weaning ourselves from the institutional succor that had kept Steve alive. Weightless in the water, Steve could practice taking steps against a gentler gravitational pull. Without the help of therapists, I would be the one to help him put one foot in front of the other, moving toward our new life together.

It took hours to get ready for these excursions. Getting Steve in and out of a swimsuit, let alone in and out of the pool, was a complex logistical and acrobatic feat. My arms ached with trying to lift and manipulate his weighty limbs to get in and out of his clothes in the cramped quarters of the handicapped changing room. When he was dressed, I would wheel him to the pool where I transferred him to a special chair that could swing him out over the water and lower him in. At first I had to instruct the lifeguard to help. I could not do it on my own. Once in the water, however, Steve was standing, as if it were normal for him to be upright. I would stand in front of him, relishing his now unaccustomed height, as he leaned into me, hands on my shoulders. As we walked together slowly in the water, Steve making each step with great effort and concentration, we could not help grinning at each other. We luxuriated in the shared and gentle movement. Surprisingly, the depth of grief that we had tasted together had carved within us a deep well that could also hold a greater depth of joy. It was not difficult to generate, spilling easily from everyday moments into our receptive hearts. Like the warm water surrounding us in the pool, it held us up.

We were daily amazed by these moments of grace, proliferating in such a seemingly hostile environment. Anne Lamott wrote in *Traveling Mercies*, "I do not understand the mystery of grace—only that it meets us where we are and does not leave us where it found us." [1] As I considered our journey thus far, the dry desert wandering, the flash floods, and the dusty mining through inhospitable terrain, I knew that we had been delivered into a territory that would leave us profoundly and mysteriously and—by grace alone—gloriously changed. This was the odd and unexpected sweetness that softened the bitterness of loss. When I say that we were and would continue to be gloriously changed, I mean it in the biblical sense: the weight and heft of what is really important was being sifted in our souls, uncovering a sacred joy, a spiritual vivacity that can blossom in the most unexpected places, like a flower in concrete. This is a grace that is there for the finding in every moment of our every day. And often, like the moments in the pool, Steve and I found it. Grace is gift. We could not manufacture it. Nor did it explain or change or erase what was painful. But it sifted and transformed us, when we allowed it, with a strange sweetness. My prayer then was that we would continue to let it carry us with gentle movements to places that we could not yet imagine.

---

[1] Anne Lamott, *Traveling Mercies: Some Thoughts on Faith* (New York: Anchor Books, 2000), p. 143.

24

DAWN

OCT 80

A picture from our walk together.

———◆———

My soul waits for the Lord
more than watchmen for the morning,
more than watchmen for the morning.

(Psalm 130:6)

In our former life in Manila, Steve would walk and pray. If he was preaching on Sunday, I knew that on Saturday night, and often on Friday night as well, he would be gone, circling our neighborhood for hours. Sometimes I would join him on these mini-expeditions, and we would walk and talk and pray together, holding hands.

In the early years of marriage, in the Pacific Northwest, we also walked on dates. We took hikes into a park and along a beach, or on more ambitious days, up small mountains or hillsides outside the city. Pausing to rest, we would lean into each other, drinking in the presence of mind achieved by our satisfied bodies, the deliciousness of rest after exertion. Often a vista would be our reward, some unfolding combination of water and mountains and sky. Sometimes we would have a picnic, lolling in the sun, before the long hike down. With the advent of children, our walks became shorter, belabored by a baby on the back or a toddler's staccato: running, stopping, looking, sitting, running, walking. But we always walked.

It was hard to believe that Steve would never again know this essential thing, this life-giving rhythm of movement, the sweet exhaustion of a body satiated, the rewards of remote vistas. It was hard to imagine that we would no longer explore a path or a park or a hillside together. Was not this movement, this exploration, this physical participation in our environment, life itself? Already, I could not recall what it was like to have a husband who could walk, who could lift up the kids and wrestle them down, who could carry heavy loads, who could lovingly grab and hold me. These were among the losses that rolled up onto our shores over and over again like a ceaseless tide. Weeks, months, years hence we would continue to bump up against the desire to be alive with movement, together.

One day, we headed out. I put on my long neglected sneakers and jogging pants and tucked a blanket around Steve's legs against the autumn chill. Our temporary home was near the ocean, where a long road with a sidewalk wound along the shoreline, ending with a view of the Puget Sound and a park. Steve wheeled along at a rapid pace. I found it hard to keep up, but I didn't care. With him rolling beside me, I was especially grateful for the ache I could feel in my legs. Finally, the road emerged from the residential cover of trees and yards and houses, and we reached a place where the ocean was unmasked, stretching out before us. I had been too intent on our pace to notice the stunning view, but now Steve stopped his chair. We paused, Steve shifting his chair in the direction of the water with an easy flick of his wrist on the joystick. I caught my breath. This was no rugged path or remote mountainside, but the scene was stunning nevertheless, here on the concrete.

With paralysis comes poor circulation and even worse temperature regulation. Steve was quickly growing cold in the chill air that now blew without obstruction from the ocean. Affectionately, I set my hat on his head, tugging it close around his ears. Then I sat on his lap and we prayed, looking out at the magnificent vista. The sun was already bright at that midday hour, but it was as if we were sitting in the barely visible rays of dawn. It was another moment of promise, each one carefully gathered up, that the dark night of longing and desire would not last forever, that there were joys to be had while we waited.

25

STUMBLING INTO JOY

SEP 80

A place to watch.

———————◆———————

Now to him who is able to do far more abundantly than all that we ask or think, according to the power that is at work within us, to him be the glory....

(Ephesians: 3:20-21)

As our confidence grew and our circle of excursions widened, we decided to attempt a trip to the beach. We had heard of one in our neighborhood that had wheelchair access, so we lowered the ramp on our van, piled Steve and the kids inside, and embarked upon our next small adventure.

The road to the park curled along a wooded cliff, down toward the sea. We parked at the bottom near the ranger's lodge and found a concrete path that wound among tall fir trees and grass toward the water. Steve wheeled along at a leisurely pace, the boys running ahead, eager to play in the sand. We were unexpectedly pulled up short, however, by a four-inch lip that separated the concrete path we had so easily traversed and a wooden bridge that crossed underneath the railroad tracks running between the forest and the beach. I heaved with all my strength but could not get the weighty electric wheelchair over it. After repeated fruitless attempts, I miserably considered leaving Steve there in the park, unable to even glimpse the water and the beach beyond. The thought felt unbearable, and I decided instead that we should all go home, rather than leave him behind. Just as we were giving up a stranger stopped to help. Together we tugged and hefted the cumbersome chair, until suddenly Steve was once again mobile on top of the bridge.

From the bridge, the tunnel underneath the tracks framed an image of ocean and sand and driftwood, beckoning us onward through the dark. As we stepped into the light at the tunnel's end, the wooden pathway stopped and a riot of nature began: a sandy peninsula that edged its blunt finger into the ocean, providing unencumbered 180-degree views of water and mountains beyond. Green wooded hills bent over us from behind.

Steve stopped at the edge of the path. The natural undulations of earth and sand and rock were not made for the inflexible aluminum and iron of his chair. Without hesitation, the children ran onto the beach, shouting. I wavered there at its edge, feeling the now familiar tension between my husband and my boys. Steve squeezed my hand and urged me forth. I had no choice but to proceed. Our two-year-old needed careful watching around all of that water.

I took a picture first, from the tunnel into the light. Steve's chair filled the frame, with all of nature spreading out before it. In the light, our children were playing. It was a poignant image of our family as it was, then. The chair had been a vehicle of freedom, but now it revealed itself as a prison as well, a walled-in room. We with legs that walk moved forward while Steve was left behind. He made the best of it, my darling husband. He sat and smiled, enjoying our pleasure, listening to a sermon on his iPod while the boys and I explored the wild shoreline. Soon my sons were running farther and farther down the beach. As I followed, I wondered if Steve could see us. His world had narrowed like the tunnel. He sat on its edge, perched between darkness and light. As we wheeled back toward the car, he said to me, "Now I have even more incentive to walk."

The opportunity came sooner than we had expected. The next day, during a physical therapy appointment, the therapist suggested the parallel bars. This could mean only one thing: the bars were made for standing... and walking. Steve could not yet stand on his own outside of water, still needing support and assistance, and yet the therapist was asking him to walk. With paralysis, each level of improvement is less like a natural progression and more like hurtling from one realm of possibility to another.

I had a secret prayer tucked away in my heart. Our tenth anniversary was coming in December, and I asked for a bold and audacious gift: that Steve would take a few steps on that day. On that morning, I added another: "Lord, if you do intend for Steve to walk, please encourage us today. Give us a glimpse of your promise."

Steve wheeled over to the bars. The therapist helped him stand and grip the bars much as he would grip our kitchen sink during his daily exercises. Steve braced himself against the therapist, who was supporting his body and offering advice, but nothing could have prepared him for this command: "Now, walk!" Steve hurtled himself over the edge of what was possible and picked up his leg and put it down just a little farther away. Then, slowly, he shifted his weight and arms, and leaned into the therapist, and did it again. And again. And again. Now he was picking up speed and he was walking. He was walking! I was crying and laughing at the same time. "You're not supposed to do this until our tenth anniversary," I chided. It was only September.

Even in the desert, God can show His abundance. He comes in pillars of fire and clouds of glory. He brings forth water from rock and provides manna with the morning dew. Steve walked the bars not once but three times on that first day. I was in awe.

I wondered if the Israelites had paused in wonder when the water flowed from the rock, or had they simply rushed to slake their thirst? I had been to the desert once, in Israel. As I stepped out of the cool shelter of our air-conditioned bus into the arid heat, I felt a pang of sympathy for the Israelites, who endured the heat and dust for years without reprieve, wandering through the monotonous days between their deliverance from Egypt and the Promised Land. At a safe distance, it was easy to see the miracle, the abundance. But under the blazing sun, upon the scorched earth, it might be easy to forget.

For now, I was drinking. The fountain was running over and the water tasted delicious. But in the morning, the bowel program would resume. The wheelchair would remain. For a moment the tunnel widened and we caught a glimpse of the promised land. Would we remember the miracle? Would we allow grace and abundance to frame our desert days? All I knew was that today He had given exceedingly more than I had asked for and had done far more than I could imagine. For a moment Steve was joining me in wide, open space. We drank in air and light and promise. We stumbled into joy.

26

NEW EVERY MORNING

OCT 80

The steadfast love of the Lord never ceases;
his mercies never come to an end;
they are new every morning;
great is your faithfulness.

(Lamentations 3:22-23)

It was already the first of November. The trees were a riot of colors, and even the bamboo planted around our house was shifting shades to match the cold, wet season. The day before, we had carved pumpkins and gone trick-or-treating with the boys, making memories out of our new American life. Dressing now required additional and unaccustomed layers of sweaters, vests, and jackets. I had to hide the shorts from the boys so that they would pull on their new and unaccustomed long pants. Zephyr, my youngest, still refused to wear socks most days, such a strange sensation for his previously unfettered feet. The next day, our firstborn would turn nine years old.

Much was also changing in Steve's body. Though he still spent the majority of his day in a wheelchair, during his therapy sessions, he now practiced walking with crutches or a cane, as well as with the now usual walker. After a mix-up that forced us to try to get into a friend's house via two stairs, Steve also began practicing stairs. Stairs! Less dramatic but equally astounding was the progress in Steve's hands. His thumb could now bend over to touch not just his middle finger but his ring finger, and almost his pinky. Strength, though elusive, was returning. His grip and pinch were getting stronger.

As time wore on, the prospect of a plateau loomed. Steve's hope became ever more fragile even as the likelihood of its realization grew. The closer he came to his desires, the more difficult it was to consider any possible defeat. While he was now able to walk, each step required all of his effort and concentration, the strain causing pain to course throughout his body. Walking was not like riding a bike. He could not remember how to do it. As he tried to improve, he had to analyze the mechanics of it. How much should he lift his foot? Did he push off with the ball of his foot or the heel? Should his calves be activated or his hamstrings? While the rest of us cheered and were amazed, Steve soberly managed his hope under all of the careful learning and the oppressive weight of pain and gravity. He looked to each day's mountain and climbed it doggedly. To look too far ahead to the next peak was simply too much to hope for and sustain, so he gave thanks for each small sign of progress and went to bed each night fortifying himself for what the next day would bring.

I tried to keep his pace. When the hope in me quickened and I wanted to stretch for that finish line, I looked over at him and slowed to a more consistent gait—more appropriate for the middle stretch of a marathon. I stopped to imagine the parade of hours he faced, the weight he strained against in order to move the smallest finger or shift his hips, and the continuing humbling process of being washed and dressed by another. And I imagined that fragile hope he carried, that thirsty little flame that he quietly, faithfully laid at the Lord's feet each day.

Scripture continued to come to mind in this, the middle stretch, to coax me forward. On that day, Lamentations 3:19-24 pressed itself upon my spirit. After descriptions of terrible affliction, the prophet declares that his peace and hope are gone. It is in the context of utter hopelessness and discouragement that he calls to mind his hope. One senses that he does not feel it but rather declares it over himself: "The steadfast love of the Lord never ceases, his mercies never come to an end;

they are new every morning; great is your faithfulness."

Remember, O my soul! Have faith! Trust! Faith is a gift, but at times it is also a discipline and a choice. Steve's daily practice was a drill, a relentless requirement to which he bowed. These days faith required similar commitment and effort. At night we laid it down and in the morning we picked it up again. For Steve, his physical practice merged with his spiritual practice. Steve put on his daily faith and bent a finger and lifted a leg, and with each step, he was saying, "Great is your faithfulness."

27

A RADIANT BRIDE

Worshipping with our faith community before Steve speaks.

---◆---

Some men came, bringing to him a paralyzed man, carried by four of them. Since they could not get him to Jesus because of the crowd, they made an opening in the roof above Jesus by digging through it and then lowered the mat the man was lying on. When Jesus saw their faith, he said to the paralyzed man, "Son, your sins are forgiven.

(Mark 2:3-5)

Our Seattle church held an event in our honor, a night of worship and prayer and fundraising. Steve's old friends from his worship days would take up the guitar he could no longer play, sing with strong lungs he no longer had, and lead us into God's presence. For the first time in a very long while, my pastor husband would speak.

It was evening when we bade the children goodnight and took ourselves off to church. We wheeled into the sanctuary to find it packed with people. I knew many of the faces, but not all of them. They shared one thing: they were all there for us. I looked around and began to cry. The kindness was so great that it was almost hard to bear.

I had grown up in the church and knew it well. I knew the frailty of the thing, the fragility of our efforts to mirror God's love, the myriad ways we fell short. I understood the voices of the scoffers who mocked our many hypocrisies, who triumphantly pointed out our failures. In many respects, they were right. I had known the sting of it personally. On that night, however, the church was blinding in its beauty. It was diverse, it was lovely, it was practical, it was humble, and it was united. On that night, people gathered for the sake of one, but the songs, the verses, and the themes of suffering and hope bound all of us together in our shared faith and humanity.

The room represented an outrageous abundance of care, of service, and of generosity, more than could ever be deserved or repaid. I received it only because I knew that in the giving we were all building hope together. Strangers, acquaintances, friends and family, together we were being church, and just for that moment, we were magnificent. The bride of Christ was beautiful to behold, shining in love and faith and hope.

We had missed church so much in the many months in the hospital and during the ensuing period when we were not yet confident enough to take on so colossal an outing as a Sunday morning service. The worship was therefore exceptionally sweet. Then it was Steve's turn. He wheeled up to the front. Sitting in his chair, he was at eye level with the people sitting before him. He had chosen the obvious story, the only story: the story of the paralytic. There was a phrase there that distilled the truth of our experience and of that moment: "because of their faith." Because of THEIR faith, the faith of the paralytic's friends, Jesus forgave the sins of the paralytic. And later, it was because of the doubts of the Pharisees that he healed the paralytic physically as well. The crux of the story is that in our suffering, we need each other. In matters of faith, we are inextricably bound together. Sometimes, we are even healed because of our friends.

I knew this in my bones. In the last six months, I had grasped every hand extended toward us. A great number of people had carried Steve's "mat". Sometimes, I crawled in beside Steve and rested while others pushed and shoved and sweated and hauled us up and over the roof into the presence of Jesus. Steve's physical suffering was so intense. Wasn't it beautiful of the Lord that He did not require him to prove his faith in his weakest moment? Instead, Jesus received the faith of our friends and it was enough. The grace of this was so vast, so free, I could not take it in. My heart overflowed as I listened to my husband speaking the true miracle: faith expressing itself in love, healing us through our friends.

We had planned the next moment. Here was a gift that we could give, a gift to tell our friends that their faith had been more than enough, that it had made a difference. This gift was ours, together.

I brought up Steve's walker and set it before him. The room hushed as we all watched. Steve rocked in his chair, creating momentum, and then heaved himself upward to standing. He paused to find his balance and then, slowly, he walked toward me, leaning into the metal frame of the walker. The congregation was on its feet, standing with him, laughing and crying and cheering. The gospel lived as he walked, not just in the miracle of the movement, but in the standing together, in the unity of joy and faith and love. Our fates and our faiths were wrapped up in each other, the essential truth of the paralytic passage lived out here and now in this collective act of hope and celebration.

We closed in prayer, hundreds of people flocking to the front where we were. They laid their hands on us, and those who could not reach us laid their hands on the people in front of them, a huge and varied web of care, stretching out across the room. There was a depression in the middle of this network of humanity where Steve's chair sat. Heads bowed and hands extended toward that spot. We were in the center of that sacred mesh of human hands, but Christ was at its core.

28

SOUL CLEARING

---◆---

He will be like a tree planted by water:
it sends its roots out toward a stream,
it doesn't fear when heat comes,
and its foliage remains green.
It will not worry in a year of drought
or cease producing fruit.

(Jeremiah 17:8)

In December, our basement flooded. I wandered into the kitchen early one morning after a heavy night of rain and looked outside to see a river flowing down the hill and into the yard. It collected itself and gathered speed on the garden path, forming a waterfall down the stairs into the basement. The water was flowing so fast, it turned white in places. In that brief instant of disbelief, I imagined myself whitewater rafting around the house and down those stairs.

A drain had gotten clogged by all of the dead leaves and pine needles in the yard, and from that tiny shift of natural refuse, a deluge had occurred. There was a lake where I once did my laundry, two feet deep and strewn with soggy cardboard and floating objects. I had to call a truck to pump it out.

Somehow I was undeterred by this mini disaster. My relationship to material things had shifted greatly in the aftermath of Steve's accident. Such is the welcome perspective of significant catastrophe. I wondered how long it would last. Best to get rid of as much as possible while my eyesight was clear.

With Steve upstairs, unable to help, I began the burdensome prospect of clearing out the overflowing, soggy area. Fortunately, friends from Hong Kong, Manila, and Portland happened to visit during the days that followed, and together we made quick work of it. A few precious books laid recovering in the dry heat next to the fireplace, but most of the contents of the basement were thrown away. I was utterly unfazed as mattresses, furniture, books, CDs and other moldy items made their way to the dump. These are the things you can't take with you.

Rangers have discovered that natural fires are necessary for healthy forest growth. For years they mistakenly protected the forests from those fires. The undergrowth became cluttered, and too many trees blocked the sunlight from reaching the forest floor. The accumulation of growth actually caused an increase in high-intensity forest fires. Now these same rangers purposely light low-intensity fires, thinning small trees and clearing vegetative debris. The forest needs a regular burning.

My soul had been similarly routed. My insides, like my basement, had been ruthlessly cleared. I was left with a stark and uncluttered space, a clear vantage point. Though the process was painful, I could sense the health and wellbeing I would derive from this new perspective. My soul felt strong and there was room to breathe. Many things clamored to fill the emptiness: duty, desire, striving. I could already feel the undergrowth gathering itself once more beneath the ashes. Like the leaves, if I allowed them to pile up for too long, they would clog up my thoughts and cause more flooding.

Faith requires that we regularly burn away the debris. Like the seed that must die in order to grow, it continually calls us to lay down life in order to find it. In forsaking what we think we want or need, we find we have more room to stretch our spirits. Our roots grow deep and then wide. Christ did it perfectly. Stumbling, we follow.

I cannot say Steve's accident was a gift. But with fire came the opportunity for new growth. Life was not quenched beneath the ashes. The peculiar logic of God's law, mirrored so aptly in nature, says that only through death can we find life.

Our fear of suffering fights against what we know to be true. Though we rarely have the courage to willingly surrender to the fire, it comes nevertheless, a providential clearing. What can fill a new space without clogging it? I moved in and out of clarity. There were things that did not clutter, even when they filled: grace, light, freedom, love, hope, forgiveness. Like oxygen, they were invisible but life-giving, pervasive yet unrestrictive.

Our basement felt lighter after the flood. Doing laundry, I watched a thin beam of light illuminate the dust motes gently floating in the new space. As I bent my head to clear the low beam at the entrance, I looked back. There was no regret. Already I had forgotten all that had filled this space. I sensed the strength of beams and walls. It was far more difficult to cast off our old life, and yet it had been cast off. Beneath the ashes something new would rise. Some day.

29

OLD

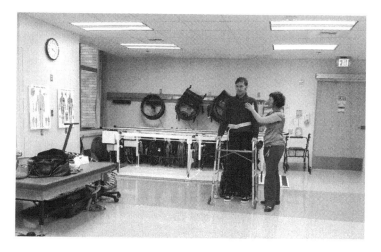

Steve doing therapy at Harborview.

Even to your old age I am he,
and to gray hairs I will carry you.
I have made, and I will bear;
I will carry and will save.

(Isaiah 46:4)

Steve's progress began to move faster and faster, making a more meaningful impact on our lives. Steve was shifting more and more toward using a walker. Where in the past it took all of Steve's energy to walk for perhaps thirty minutes out of an entire 24-hour day, he now often grabbed his walker or his manual chair to move around the house. For two whole days, he stayed out of his power chair entirely. His confidence and strength had grown so much that we managed several outings without any wheelchair at all.

Without the wheelchair life felt much more normal. Steve could sit in a regular car, he could ride an escalator, he could access public bathroom stalls, and he could sit in church pews, movie theater seats, and restaurant booths. Of course, getting up and down and in and out of all of these remained a challenge, but so far we had managed.

We often joked during this period that we were practicing for old age. The patience amidst the slow pace of life, the endurance through the body's breakdowns, and the humbling dependence on others was an apt rehearsal for our twilight years.

One day during a visit to Harborview, Steve saw an elderly man walking with a walker and commented that he looked like him. "No, honey," I honestly replied, "he looks better than you!" Still, for us, this slow and awkward navigation of short distances from car to destination felt like the euphoric sprint at the end of a long race.

Having been forced to slow to an almost impossibly laborious pace in the wheelchair, we cherished the freedom and relative speed and spontaneity with which we were more and more able to participate in normal life. We were young, but we had become accustomed to a life so circumscribed by Steve's limitations, that these small freedoms produced a burst of energy and hope like that of a long distance runner when the finish line comes into sight. While we understood that the end was still far off, we felt the wind at our back and the promise of a better destination ahead.

While there was a relative ease to our days, we had to remain doggedly disciplined with the small freedoms we enjoyed. Steve stuck to a strict regimen of therapies and stretching exercises, supplements and bowel and bladder routines that made these bits of progress possible. When we stretched too far too fast, Steve's body collapsed in exhaustion and often illness. We had to pay attention to the constantly shifting terrain, and were often at a loss as we sought the way forward.

It is difficult to explain how God carried us, except that He did. We could not quite explain how we had gotten there or why the air tasted so fresh despite the many temptations toward despair. There was a strange sense of protection and of holy calling on this road. God continued to fold His wings around us in a sheltering embrace. On a drive to the airport to pick up a friend, I suddenly found myself weeping, not with sadness but with tears of joy and gratitude at the loving presence we felt so deeply each day. In my mind's eye I imagined a radiant joy streaming down toward me, offering riches far beyond our circumstances. While the disciplines of life remained, a promise also planted itself in our hearts.

30

A SOUL ENLARGED

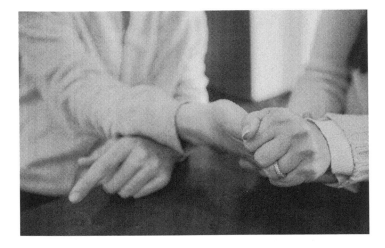

Stretching out Steve's stiff fingers to keep them limber.

———— ◆ ————

For as we share abundantly in Christ's sufferings,
so through Christ we share abundantly in comfort too.

(2 Corinthians 1:5)

Each week brought a greater measure of independence. One day Steve told me he wanted to drive again. I looked at him, incredulous. But when the specialty instructor came to test him, he determined not only that Steve was capable of driving himself, but that he needed no special instruments to assist him in manipulating a car. Never mind that he could barely get into and out of the seat!

The day came when Steve could drive himself to his therapy appointments. These solo excursions were carefully measured by his limited abilities. There were certain requirements: close parking, a short walking distance, easy access to bathrooms. In the beginning, he only drove alone to places with health care professionals who could assist him upon arrival, should he need it. Nevertheless, this was an amazing level of freedom and autonomy for Steve.

Curiously, as the clamor of insistent needs died down, I felt a deep undercurrent of grief quietly reasserting itself. As the pressure to survive began to lift, grief trickled through the cracks into the empty spaces it left behind. Quietly, the tiny drops collected into little pools. Urgency abated and my grip on faith became less desperate and sure. I wavered in my certainty.

Until now the present had been all consuming. I had neither time nor mental space to imagine our former life. I was in a new country both literally and figuratively, living under a host of new rules and limitations, learning the language of quadriplegia. The old way of being was on such a distant shore that it seemed surreal in the light of our current circumstances. I had difficulty imagining my formerly athletic, vibrant husband who tackled and tossed my children, easily dove into a pool, walked around our village for hours praying and doing sermon preparation, and loved to go hiking. I was entirely absorbed in who Steve was in the present and what he needed to get well. But as the spaces in our lives and hearts grew beyond mere survival, I found the specter of who Steve was visiting me at surprising moments, moving me to tears. I tried to accept and even welcome this new wave of sadness, not because I wanted to dwell in self-pity or wallow in what was lost, but because every expert suggested that the best way forward must be through the grief and not around it.

There had been only one consistent pattern to our grief: constant adjustment. The happy fact of Steve's progress also meant that we were forever adjusting our lives. We lived amid a pile of medical paraphernalia, surrounded by a complex web of intertwining schedules. These were forever being tweaked, discarded, and acquired according to Steve's evolving abilities. The Hoyer lift now thankfully sat in the garage, making space for a stationary bicycle. Steve's automatic wheelchair was accompanied by a spiffy scooter. There were walkers and crutches and canes strewn throughout the house like so many fallen branches after a storm. Our lovely bathroom was still marred by the ever-present shower chair, but perhaps not for long. Therapies were similarly in flux, not to mention our emotions. When people asked me about my grief process, my best answer was that I didn't know what I'd lost yet. Certainly, there had been profound losses during these many months, but the scope of them was completely unascertainable.

One of the books by my bedside was a book by Jerry Sittser called *A Grace Disguised*. I had read parts of it long ago, with great compassion but only minimal understanding, given that the circumstances were so much more devastating than anything I had previously known. Professor Sittser had lost his mother, wife, and youngest child in a brutal car accident. The book was an honest, thoughtful account of grief and loss alongside a loving and gracious God. As I read it again, one passage struck me in relation to our own experience: "... (T)ragedy can increase the soul's capacity for darkness and light, for pleasure as well as for pain, for hope as well as for dejection... (The soul) can grow larger through suffering. Loss can enlarge its capacity for anger, depression, despair, and anguish, all natural and legitimate emotions when we experience loss. Once enlarged, the soul is also capable of experiencing greater joy, strength, peace and love.... the soul is capable of experiencing these opposites, even at the same time." [2]

As I let the grief come, I found it did not negate the grace we'd built in so many everyday moments together. At times the loss loomed large, like when I remembered how Steve used to play the guitar, creating a silly song out of a comment I made, making the children laugh. His musician's fingers were unlikely to ever play an instrument again. Such grief deserved to be mourned and yet there was little chance to dwell there. The good kept bumbling in. Our two-year-old was ever present,

[2] Gerald L. Sittser, *A Grace Disguised: How the Soul Grows Through Loss* (Grand Rapids, Michigan: Zondervan Pub. House, 1996), p. 48.

wanting to play. I could not resist the surge of wellness that came from the sweet-smelling folds of his neck or the ready giggles when we tickled him. The older boys were equally geared toward living, with dance parties in the kitchen (Steve grooving in his chair), and games of tag in the yard.

I was rarely allowed the luxury of a single emotion. Instead they piled one upon the other, a complex fusion of happiness and grief. As Professor Sittser described, there was a richness to the mix, marked by hearts expanded by grief to hold greater amounts of joy.

31

GLORY DRAWS NEAR

Our family Christmas card photo, 2010.

———— ◆ ————

He said to me, "My grace is sufficient for you,
for my power is made perfect in weakness."

(2 Corinthians 12:9)

Advent came, a season of waiting and longing for God to draw near. Contrary to the frantic activity proposed by Christmas culture, God asks us to slow down, to dwell in anticipation, to stoop low in order to catch his humble appearance.

The babe in the manger looked different to me now. I was more tender toward His weak estate. God became incarnate in a symbol of utmost vulnerability, placing Himself at our mercy. I could almost see His jugular offered up, His life blood flowing, naked and unprotected.

The babe elicits tenderness. Its weakness makes us want to shield it. Thus, weakness draws forth strength. That protective impulse, that tenderness over weakness is, I believe, an imperfect but true reflection of the Godhead. In Isaiah 40, God tenderly gathers his lambs in his arms, pressing them to his bosom. Is not the babe a stunning reversal of that very impulse? Now it is we who tenderly lift the babe, our God, into our arms, pressing him to our chests. There is no greater cry for relationship than this dance of weakness and strength, one covering the other with tenderness and mercy and grace. The babe, once weak, grows up and covers us in turn, His victory achieved through weakness. Once more, the jugular is exposed. This time He fails to draw protection. The blood runs, and in that most stunning and mysterious of eternal equations, this very weakness is strength.

A particular ministry is born out of our weakness. That ministry is simply to allow others in, to allow God in. The challenge is not to cover it, not to hide the truth about ourselves. Instead, we allow God and others to bend over us and draw us near. Fragile and unguarded, we are drawn closer. Somehow, light streams forth from the cracks.

That December we were vulnerable. We needed help to grasp the mystery. We needed reminders of the miracle. Like the forgotten babe in the stable, visitors found us and brought worship to our humble estate. One day, an especially random hodgepodge of folk entered our kitchen, strangers to each other. Friends from Manila joined our two caregivers and ourselves around our simple table, a fire crackling in the fireplace. Soon, they began to sing Christmas songs. It just so happened that these folk all meant what they were singing. It also just so happened that they had an unusually high level of musical talent among them. The traditional songs of the season took on new meaning as we sang out loud the hope of Advent together. Steve and I added our weaker voices to their beautiful harmonies and for an hour or more, that simple room resounded with praise, the ordinary transcending its bounds and touching a greater glory.

Glory draws near in humble form. That is the miracle of Christmas. That year I knew it to be true. Our need had drawn those disparate people to us, and our hardship softened our hearts to each other in ways that strength never could. In that fellowship of suffering and care, we received His glory more profoundly. God inhabited our weakness with His grace, and from that grace emerged a powerful moment of strength. It emerged when we came together with our frailty exposed, remembering a God who was well acquainted with weakness, the God of the universe who was also a babe in a manger. He drew near that Christmas in ways we might never know again, because we might never be that weak again, and brought the gift of Himself. No gift would ever be more precious or profound.

32

TOGETHER IN THE FIRE

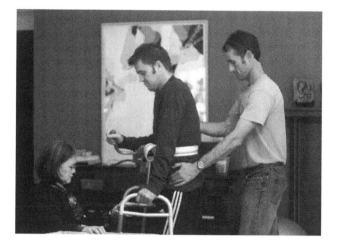

---

*Then King Nebuchadnezzar was astonished and rose up in haste.
He declared to his counselors, "Did not we cast three men bound
into the fire?" They answered and said to the king, "True, O king."
He answered and said, "But I see four men unbound, walking in the
midst of the fire, and they are not hurt; and the appearance of the
fourth is like a son of the gods."*

(Daniel 3:24-25)

The sight of Steve on his feet became more and more familiar. The distance from one room to another was still all that he could manage with the assistance of a cane or walker. He moved slowly, shambling, and sat quickly, falling into chairs. The deep seat of the couch in front of the TV was particularly challenging. I tried to help him up one day and could not seem to heave hard enough. We fell back laughing. Steve and I sat there together until our caregiver arrived to help.

We began to measure his progress by rooms. First, from the bedroom to the kitchen, the longest distance in our house. Next Trader Joe's, a smallish store down the street. Then QFC, slightly larger. Grocery carts made excellent makeshift walkers. We dreamt of conquering Costco, that huge warehouse store, a seemingly unimaginable vastness.

Walking should have been a joy, but it was not. The freedom it permitted was heady and wonderful, but the act itself was burdensome, full of striving. It never felt good, each step requiring massive effort. Steve was like a professional weight lifter manipulating barbells around his legs. I imagined the red-faced tension I had seen on TV, the athlete's body straining and heaving in order to exact the smallest movement. This was the effort it took Steve to stand, let alone heave his weighty limbs.

When we are stuck in life, hardship often causes much needed movement. Pain wakes us up and demands that we respond. In the classic Bible story, Shadrach, Meshach and Abednego are thrown into a fire for refusing to bow down to an idol. The ropes that bind them are burned away in the flames, and yet the three young men are seen walking in the fire. The fire with which Steve and I had been tested had freed us from the encumbrances of possessions, habits, and security. As these were burned away, our spirits had been loosened from their moors. In response to the burning, we had moved halfway around the world. All of this hurt, but the pain caused us to pay attention.

Loosed from so many material constraints, we looked with a keener spiritual awareness, and saw that we were not alone in this fire. It seems an easy observation. The words are hackneyed and often abused, delivered as cheap consolation to some wrecked heart: "You are not alone." But this was holy ground. A son of god was loosed into the burning, unperturbed by the fiery coals. We understood that in the midst of the burning, God was doing something holy and miraculous.

In therapy, they helped Steve lie on the floor and then asked him to get up. The first few times he could not do it, hauling and wrestling his weak appendages into all manner of awkward positions. He looked like a squashed spider squirming under an invisible weight. But one day, he did it, coming up red-faced from exertion but beaming with triumph.

In the biblical story, the men were untouched, not even the smell of smoke lingering in their hair. Our children were like them, joyfully playing, seemingly unhindered by the flames. Steve and I still choked on the smoke. We got dirty in the ashes. But we were moving in the furnace. While we did not relish this burning, Someone was moving with us in the fire, and we were aware of a holy presence among us.

33

GATHERED INTO ARMS

Steve surprised me on our tenth wedding anniversary
with a visit to the chapel where he had proposed.

———— ◆ ————

For everything there is a season,
and a time for every matter under heaven:

...a time to weep and a time to laugh;
a time to mourn and a time to dance.

(Ecclesiastes 3:1, 4)

It seemed a lifetime ago that I had held the prayer out. I had asked that Steve would take a few steps on our 10th anniversary. Already my hands were overflowing with the answer. Audaciously, I asked for more: *Lord, might we dance?*

Ten years ago I had married my love. Not one for milestones or chocolate or flowers or fancy dinners, I had uncharacteristically attached particular significance to this tenth year. The number felt broad and tall, our first time in double digits, symbolic of a love that had endured through the many highs and lows we had weathered together. I was proud of us. Before the accident, I had dreamed of a trip to Africa or some other far-flung adventure to celebrate. Now I didn't care where we would go. I just want my husband to hold me and sway a little

Our anniversary arrived on a cold, clear day in December. We had booked dinner in a fancy restaurant with dear friends and a hotel room, while Steve's parents watched our kids. I had carefully enquired about wheelchair accessibility, and packed the many accoutrements we still needed to meet Steve's needs. We went back and forth about bringing the wheelchair. It made Steve feel helpless, returning to the chair, but the city blocks between hotel and restaurant were long. Cold was difficult. He could not feel the low temperatures, but his muscles responded with a tightening that hampered his ability to walk. Whatever walking might occur would be more arduous. In the end, we played it safe and I was glad as I snuggled into his lap on the way to the restaurant, cruising along the sidewalk in his chair.

Returning to our room that night, there was a simplicity

to what lay ahead. In the past, renting a hotel room for just the two of us would entail the promise of a physical intimacy that was no longer possible. The range of delights had been radically reduced. Steve had planned a gift more precious than any we had previously known, however. He had prepared a song about grace, the one we had played on our wedding day. Pressing play, he wheeled the chair up to me and turned it off. With a great heave, he pulled himself up and held out his arms. I entered his circle and leaned in. We swayed gently, just a few rounds. The song ended and we went to sleep.

The body is finite but the soul is infinite. It can hold two opposing experiences separated by a seemingly limitless expanse, along with countless variations in between. On the one hand, we were plummeting into a cavernous hole of what was lost and on the other we stood with arms outstretched upon a mountain of blessing. For those who lose someone or something precious, holidays and special events are the hardest because they underscore the loss. For us there was an element of this as well. Anniversaries, vacations, times of celebration would only bring into focus what daily life allowed us to ignore. We could not celebrate the same. And yet, where hope and trust remains, the helplessness of falling need not cancel out the sweetness of what has been given. On that particular day we stretched ourselves across the boundless distance between those opposite poles, both lost in the depths and rejoicing on the mountain top. In touching both we found a peculiar balance.

There is indeed a season for everything, however, no season is one singular thing, though some notes may play louder than others. Our dance was the most tender of motions—awkward, weak, yet utterly given, one to the other. We danced equal parts joy and sorrow. We danced autumn and spring, the seasons that are in between. The contrast provided its own kind of beauty, like the clashing colors of fall leaves. Among the dying leaves, there were buds yet to blossom. God stretched beyond time and easily encompassed the extremes of our experience. Our souls, tasting His surrounding and eternal embrace, rested in His everlasting arms.

34

PROGRESS LOOKS LIKE THIS

Steve and I at a concert together.

◆

For now we see in a mirror dimly, but then face to face.
Now I know in part; then I shall know fully,
even as I have been fully known.

(1 Corinthians 13:12)

Sometimes we failed to recognize how far we had come on this journey. We took our cues from those who saw us only sporadically. Steve's progress was more accurately mirrored in their astonishment and delight. It was indeed a miracle, but in the seemingly uneventful wasteland between acute care and normal life, Steve and I sometimes lost our vantage point.

And yet, the progress was measurable and real. Target and even Costco were now possible to navigate, albeit with great effort and determination. Thanks to the shopping cart, one might never notice the extent of Steve's limitations. Most happily, Steve had regained a significant amount of bowel control, which ushered in a whole new level of independence and dignity, as well as eliminating much of the arduous morning routine.

In the past few weeks, wrestling had returned to our house. This was, of course, a favorite pastime for our three young boys, especially with their papa. Steve deeply grieved the loss of his ability to connect with our boys this way, and so the slow return of strength and agility that allowed him to brokenly resume roughhousing had been a treat. This time, it was a more cautious choreography. Nevertheless, I frequently heard giggles erupting from the bedroom where Steve winsomely pretended to be ferocious despite his relative weakness. The boys were delighted and gladly played along within the soft and forgiving confines of our bed.

These were no small victories in the world of spinal cord injury. Even among our few "walking quad" acquaintances, ours were rare milestones of progress. It was sobering that even among the star recoveries, all of them had some permanent level of compromised function. One day I joined in the reckless fray of wrestling, only to find that I had lost my best defense. Steve was no longer ticklish, with only negligible sensation in his armpits. This was how I discovered that in fact his altered sensation began much higher on his body than I had realized, just below the top of his shoulders.

Such were the mixed moments, both the delights and the intrusions of reality that made up daily life somewhere between injury and healing. We hoped for the best even as we prepared to accept whatever we were given.

35

GRASPING FAITH

Walking on the beach where once he had perched at its edge, limited by his chair.

———•◆•———

I will remember the deeds of the Lord;
yes, I will remember your wonders of old.
I will ponder all your work,
and meditate on your mighty deeds.
Your way, O God, is holy.
What god is great like our God?
You are the God who works wonders;
you have made known Your might among the peoples.

(Psalm 77:11-14)

Even as Steve improved, I found myself questioning the possibility of complete healing. The daily rhythm of his handicap had taken shape, solidifying into an unavoidable reality. Much of the time I was too busy to notice, until I suddenly found myself in the shadow of something all too real. One day, as I sensed the shadow of despair descending, I retreated into our bedroom to pray.

The room was like a cave, its thick brown rug and low ceiling creating a dark and sheltering space, looking out through many windows to green. I tucked myself into our special bed with its automated elevation system, my bible in my lap. Praying, I confessed my uncertainty, giving God my ebbing faith for healing. "Lord, I don't know how to pray anymore. I confess that I'm no longer certain that you will heal Steve completely. Will you?" As I prayed, I found myself led into the Psalms, that perfect prayer book for the desperate. Seeking comfort there, I read an unfamiliar psalm. "I cry aloud to God, aloud to God, and he will hear me. In the day of my trouble I seek the Lord; in the night my hand is stretched out without wearying, my soul refuses to be comforted." Indeed, my soul found little comfort.

Restlessly, still praying, I moved on. I picked up a Bible study CD that had languished for months by my bed. I sought out the next lecture and pressed play. It opened with words from the very psalm I had just read, centering on a verse I had overlooked. "You are the God who works wonders." The teacher spoke specifically about trusting God for miracles, especially miracles of physical healing.

Is this how God answers? In the tiny coincidences? What

were the chances that I would read the psalm on which she would preach? How likely was it that the topic would answer the very question troubling my heart? My heart overflowed onto my cheeks, speaking gratitude and trust. It said, *He hears me.* I chose to open my heart to the words.

God reveals himself in glimpses such as these. At times we think the Bible full of miracles and forget that for the recipients, these blasting illustrations of God's power are few and far between, great punctuations in the otherwise mundane trajectories of their lives. Christians and Jews the world over cling to the same ancient tales of wonder. The Passover, the parting of the Red Sea, the exodus. We tell the same stories again and again. We weave belief out of ancient history, out of the miracles of others. For the most part, in our daily lives, He gives only enough, that we who are free to choose may exercise our faith, our discipline, our trust in order to find what we seek. Such is the burden of freedom. God chooses not to overpower us, but gives us space to approach. Extending his arm, he invites but does not command our friendship, let alone our worship.

Nor are we allowed to rely on equations: if I believe, then He will do this for me. He is God; we cannot make Him bend to our will. There are promises of which we are assured from the mouth of God Himself, but so often the facts and figures of our lives do not neatly fit the biblical principles. Our desires are neither small nor meaningless. Will Steve walk? Might his fingers once more caress? Can we know again the intimacies of marriage? These things matter, even to God Himself. He wept when Lazarus died, knowing He would bring him back mere moments later. Ultimately, we surrender not just our lives, but our understanding. We do this not because we are stupid but because we love, and we love because we have first been loved by love Himself.

Faith is a necessary ingredient to this kind of belief. Ultimately, faith does not require proof, but rather chooses to tell the story. That morning, I chose God yet again. I chose miracles and hope. In the quiet of my cave, I felt seen and heard by the Maker of All. When I chose this story, the story of a God who hears and responds, life flowed with a searing truth I sensed was real. No false comfort here, for faith required much of me. In trusting, I was stepping out on a limb that might not hold. Should it break, He would catch me, and I would yet again surrender understanding unto faith. I chose to edge out onto the branch, once again placing my trust in the One who works wonders.

As I tentatively dusted off hope and put it on once more, I hurried forth to share my tale with Steve. He nodded seriously, taking it in. There was no bright light, no voice from heaven, nor did he fall on his face in wonder. This was my story, my branch. He was higher up the tree and naked, risking all. I tucked the promise away to better hold on. The God who works wonders may or may not work this miracle upon us. In the meantime, I would follow the story to its end. And one day, perhaps, we would look back in wonder.

36

THE CORD THAT BINDS

Renewing our vows as the boys look on.

———— ◆ ————

Two are better than one... For if they fall, one will lift up his fellow.
But woe to him who is alone when he falls and has not another to lift
him up! Again, if two lie together, they keep warm, but how can one
keep warm alone? And though a man might prevail against one who is
alone, two will withstand him - a three-fold cord is not quickly broken.

(Ecclesiastes 4:9-12)

Almost a year after the accident, we renewed our marriage vows. Steve was not the same, and I had a longing to acknowledge both what was lost and what remained. What bound us together had woven itself tighter with the strain, a knot compressed by the pressure of the weight, taut and unrelenting, stronger now than before. I had a desire to celebrate, to make beautiful the tighter strands.

We returned to the place where we fell in love, a wild park on a cliff overlooking the ocean and mountains of Puget Sound. Hidden underneath an overhanging bit of earth, we had first confessed our love, Steve reading me a poem he had written. We returned an entirely different party, three children in tow, a ragged line of kin making its way through the tall grass toward the cliff and the view. Steve walked slowly and solemnly because of the effort, a walking stick in hand, like the tribal chief of our herd. I wore a simple white dress. It was just us and the photographers. We needed no other witness to this stirring scene than the God who had shaped it, the third strand in our strong cord. This strand held our two together.

Good times—whispered love poetry and gorgeous picnics—are important fuel for love, but hard times test the strength of it. When it withstands the test, it grows stronger, more durable. The youthful spontaneity, the energy, the playful explorations we had once known in that park and in another life would never be ours to hold again in quite the same way, despite the fact that we were not yet old. What surprised me, however, was that those things, though sorely missed, had become superfluous to the love that had grown from them.

We were now so bound by time and memory, by progeny and suffering, by faith and doubt, that we simply were, an entity unto itself—the whole more important than its parts.

We did not celebrate a pretty cord, nor a perfect one. The children were screaming, climbing in a tree, not at all present to the sacred moment as Steve and I repeated the words of the marriage covenant and drank from the cup. A jogger ran past. The wind caused a stray hair to stick to my lip as we leaned in to kiss. Steve was struggling to stand. We were a beautiful, awkward mess. No tangible change was felt once the vows had been said. The photographers had brought a poster that read, "Don't give up." We held up the words, posing with them under the tree. Inevitably, we would need to be reminded.

Nevertheless, something holy lived somewhere in the disarray. We sought it in our fumbling ritual and in the words that filled the air. Our marriage was bigger than our happiness, better than a poem. In simply living it, we had become it. We were complete because we were together, we three. Marriage as we understood it was not about our individual selves so much as it was about the relationship of each one to the other two. Created to reflect Christ, it bore the inevitable stamp of self-sacrifice. For what is love if not the willingness to do for the other what is not comfortable or easy or pleasurable to the self? No love is worth its merit if its gifts are cheap.

I looked back over the year and counted the cost. I chose to speak the vows once more. Standing there I acknowledged a gift more precious than my own desire. I honored a love grown thicker with adversity, more resilient with sacrifice, stronger with hardship.

37

PROMISE

————◆————

And the LORD gave Job twice as much as he had before.

(Job 42:10)

We were first married in New York City on December 30th, 2000, in the midst of a snowstorm. The city bowed to the weather and was quiet on that day, the earth matching my dress. Since then, we had managed to return almost every year to New York, the city that we loved, a pilgrimage of sorts to our younger selves, to the genesis of our union. It was not surprising, then, that I chose to return once more to that beloved city to celebrate my fortieth birthday.

Coming to New York was more than just a birthday celebration. We were re-embracing life. This was the first time since Steve's accident that we chose to do something for the pure fun of it. Though we still had to use wheelchair assistance at the airport, travel was unimaginably easier than it would have been as a quadriplegic. The taste of freedom was almost intoxicating. As we flew I felt the years coming off, shedding the worn edges fashioned by too much worry and constant diligence. When we arrived at our friends' loft, we found the scooter we had purchased and mailed to their home waiting in the entryway. This would be a less obtrusive way to mitigate the demands of walking New York's beaten pavements. We had to give up on the subway—too many steps and no assurance of a seat—but kind friends had given us money toward the trip, and we'd use that on the many cabs we would need to take when Steve tired. Despite the constant calculating of distances, the necessary medicines and paraphernalia, and the additional limitations, we embraced a sense of liberation. We were together in the city we loved and every bit of it was pure gift. It just so happened that the week that I turned forty was also the one-year anniversary of Steve's accident. We gave it little thought, not tending toward the dramatic. The Lord, however, had other plans.

It happened on the very morning of the anniversary of the accident, as I rose in our friend's beautiful loft. In the center of our view, framed perfectly by the window, was a double rainbow. I had seen them only a handful of times before. This one arced thickly from a cluster of buildings, stretching skyward and gradually losing shape on its return toward Earth, like a paintbrush running out of paint. The sun glinted brightly through it, making it golden with promise and light.

I almost stopped breathing, in awe at the exactness of it, showing up on this day of all days. In the early stages after Steve's accident, the Lord had whispered a verse to me, Job 42:10: "And the Lord gave Job twice as much as he had before." Often the promise of it would return to my heart, a tender and personal word of hope and reassurance. I sensed that the Lord would not let this suffering define the subsequent chapters of our lives. Though Job's suffering seemed pointless and severe, at its end the Lord gave him double what he had had at the beginning. While we are not assured of such happy endings in this life, I sensed a promise in those words for us. That promise reverberated through my mind and heart once more as I looked at the double rainbow, painting double hope and a double blessing across the atmosphere. As I entered my fortieth year, and on the anniversary of the accident, it said that this present suffering would not have the final word.

We all hear God differently. Rarely had I sensed more than

a general revelation of His majesty through creation. But this double rainbow felt personal, a gift for me and for Steve—outrageously abundant, shouting specific spiritual truth, springing from a living Word into my very being. It was an audacious thing to believe that the rainbow was there for Steve and for me, but I based it entirely on who I knew God to be, rather than on who I was or what I deserved.

God has always been like this, more than I could ask for or imagine. Knowing Him across a lifetime has been an ever unfolding revelation and expansion of my understanding of His love. There is an abundance to how He gives. He does not give part of Himself, but all. He does not only forgive our iniquities, He remembers them no more. He does not merely replace what is lost, He doubles it. He does not only whisper in our spirits, He paints His love across the sky. I was a person bent and shaped by this love, undone by it. I took out my camera and captured it on film, but I did not need the proof. The image was written into my heart, and inscribed on the palms of His hands. A double portion, more than I could ever ask for. We hope for what we cannot see, but on that precise day, in that exact part of the world and through that very window, hope showed itself in flagrant, unashamed color, in perfect design.

38

LOVE DELIVERS A LIFE

Steve officiating his parents' wedding.

---◆---

Therefore, be imitators of God, as beloved children.
And walk in love, as Christ loved us and gave himself up for us,
a fragrant offering and sacrifice to God.

(Ephesians 5:1-2)

In the year following Steve's accident, every waking hour had been focused on rehabilitation and healing. Now Steve's growing independence enabled us to look further ahead, picking up old responsibilities that had long seemed impossible. It was a miracle that our church in Manila had chosen to wait a whole year on the possibility of our return. Their belief that further healing might come buoyed our own, and after much prayer and discussion, we knew we were being called back into that faithful community. Yet again, we hoisted up the life we had built, depositing its material evidence in boxes bound for our former home and coaxing our hearts to follow. Beginning again involved countless decisions and a lot of travel. For two months we lived out of three suitcases in five cities. As we limped from place to place, it was difficult to absorb that our general trajectory was aimed at the life we had had before. Though the territory was familiar, we were changed. Freshly wounded, we were uncertain of our capacity to fulfill the demands we had previously shouldered with relative ease. Like the parable of the wineskins, our new selves could not be poured into our old life. A new life would have to be created to hold us. We had no idea what the new wine skin would look like and yet again we had to put our trust in the One who was calling us back.

I had to stop frequently to breathe and remember the Holy Spirit during those days of transition. I breathed best when I looked up, but I also breathed better when I looked at Steve and he looked back at me; so much of our story was bound up with each other and with the One who first breathed into us.

It was a mystery how we had become thus entwined, so that when I looked at him, it was almost as though I was looking at a part of myself. The shared experience of suffering had further narrowed the boundaries between us until being with him was as natural as being by myself, and when we were apart for even a few hours, I missed him. The old Genesis verse was working itself out in our marriage: (t)herefore a man shall leave his father and his mother and hold fast to his wife, and they shall become one flesh (Gen. 2:24). Ephesians takes it further, saying of marriage: "This mystery is profound, and I am saying that it refers to Christ and the church" (Eph. 5:31-32). Indeed, Steve's spirit did not live in me as Christ's spirit did, and yet with each passing year, our interests became more entwined, our identities more closely tied. Just as I wanted more of Christ and less of me, so also my desires for Steve's well-being grew and my desires for myself diminished. Ten years together had worn one steady path that now only occasionally diverted into two.

One special day, Steve officiated as his parents renewed their marriage vows after fifty years. A host of family and friends gathered in the same church where they had been married, to mark the years of their continuously unfolding union. Under the old beams, vows were spoken once more, and standing, Steve pronounced God's blessing on the mystery of the two made one. I yearn for that same blessing, to be allowed to grow old together, mingling our experiences, our legacy and our very selves into a more profound alliance. Should we be granted that privilege, I hope that we will not only deepen in oneness, but reflect more brilliantly the mystery that our union embodies: Christ and the church. This is a costly love, one that lays its life down. I had glimpsed the measure of its worth that year, as we both bent toward one another under the weight of our shared affliction. An equally natural inclination might have been to lean away, arriving at separate destinations, shoring ourselves up. And yet, by grace, we leaned in, opening ourselves up to the joy and sorrow of the other, stretching the confines of our own experience to absorb each other's, holding our own needs lightly. This is a counterintuitive action, to open instead of to close, to grant entrance instead of to protectively shut, to give yourself away instead of building yourself up. While there is no assurance of reciprocation, the hard work of love is worth it. The Bible says this kind of love is sanctifying, meaning that in laying ourselves down we both purify and set apart the other. The irony is that while the end result is a kind of cleanliness, sanctification is a sweaty, messy process. The work is an edification in itself, a kind of sweat lodge of the heart, shedding toxins and excess baggage in the process. However it is received, there is always refinement available in the practice.

If I had not first received this kind of love, I'm not sure I would have known how to give it. I drew from the boundless depths I had received through Christ. As my faith and understanding grew, it only expanded the borders of what was possible. If my love for Steve were but a dim reflection of the love between God and His bride, between my Savior and myself, then I would gladly give myself over to it. While breathing delivered a moment, love delivered life.

39

WALKING TOWARD THE CENTER

Back in the Philippines, November 2011.

For we know that if the tent, which is our earthly home, is destroyed,
we have a building from God, a house not made with hands, eternal in
the heavens. For in this tent we groan, longing to put on our heavenly
dwelling, if indeed by putting it on we may not be found naked. For while
we are still in this tent we groan, being burdened - not that we would be
unclothed, but that we would be further clothed, so that what is mortal
may be swallowed up by life. He who has prepared us for this very thing
is God, who has given us the Spirit as a guarantee.

(2 Corinthians 5:1-5)

I called Steve my 86-year-old man. It made it easier to explain, but the reality was that 86 years old was closer to dying than it was to living. Yet at 42 years old, 86 was the address where he lived, and where we lived together.

An eighty-six-year-old man struggles with a multitude of complaints that now belonged to Steve. His bowel and bladder gave way at inopportune moments. Sometimes a bathroom was simply too far away. He measured his destination carefully, parking the car close to the door. He moved slowly, allowing extra time for every small errand. He ate extra fiber and kept a complex regimen of pills and supplements. He no longer went out at night, being too tired. He feared falling on brittle bones, and he got sick easily and took longer to recover. He searched restaurants and churches for the softest chairs. His body always ached.

Each morning, my young-old man lay in bed and gathered up his strength. He set down youthful desire and picked up his elderly limitations. He assembled acceptance alongside grace. He rallied his courage and mustered up endurance. Like a good soldier he committed to the day and arose with discipline. Getting up was half the day's work.

On Sundays before he preached, Steve put on a diaper and his compression stockings to keep his blood pressure up. He grabbed a pillow to soften the hard pew. As he mounted the steps to the stage, he put all of his energy into not stumbling. On bad days, he had trouble focusing on his sermon because he needed to think too much about standing.

One day, he felt the need to relieve himself just as the choir was finishing its last song before the sermon. Should he stop everything in order to laboriously make his way back up the aisle to the bathroom as all eyes rested on him? It was one of those days where the distance and timing were all wrong, so he let go into the diaper, but the diaper did not hold. A pool of urine gathered on the pew around him and dripped onto the floor. His robe was soaked. Just as he perceived the diaper's malfunction, the choir finished and now it was his turn. He did not want to interrupt worship or distract the congregation, so he preached his sermon, dripping.

In a Bible study I was reading, the author talked about margins. Margins are the blank spaces that frame the crowded centers of a life and its host of duties. Ideally, we need to make room for the margins, pushing the "to do" lists into their proper place and creating boundaries that allow us room to breathe. Broad margins mean that when the duties spill over our carefully constructed protective walls, we can still maintain a sense of calm.

Our margins were slim. While we could manage most of life, the little things, like grains of sand, gradually accumulated to raise the water level to overflowing. One small thing piled upon the next: the distances at the mall, the location of the bathroom, the real pain of a hard seat on bones that were no longer protected by fat and muscle, a common cold, the necessity of sleep. These previously irrelevant details crowded into the already dense thicket of duties at the center. They overflowed the pages of Steve's life and mine. I went to bed early and woke up tired. I was less hungry and less hopeful. I committed to fewer things so that I could be with Steve. Our lives were circumscribed and our margins were spare.

When I think of growing old, I imagine the wider spaces of youth narrowing toward a more focused end. The destination is a point on the horizon. As we near it, we are less likely to stray off course. We lack both the energy and the desire to follow detours. The gathering history behind us forms a more comprehensive map. We walk more slowly but with greater intention. We pay more attention to the chosen path, to the details accumulating within our line of vision. We expend our energies carefully. We have spent many of our most crucial choices and few remain.

In our case, expanding our margins seemed impossible. Our newly constrained life could no longer conform to the normal equations people lived by. Now the open space we needed so much had to be created not at the outskirts of our lives, but at its messy center. The accident had changed the paper on which our life was written. With our margins consumed, we set our sights on the tapered point of space and light at the center, brought into focus by the encroaching limitations. We would spend more time on the narrow path. Steve would walk slowly, forced to pay attention to the details at hand. He could no longer roam freely, with copious amounts of energy to spare, examining a myriad of possibilities. I would pace myself with him because I did not want to leave him behind. Though I might wander away briefly, I would quickly return. We would walk together toward our destination.

If this life was a tent, and heaven was a building, we had pitched our tent closer to its doors. Though in reality we were no nearer the final destination, we were more aware of its inevitable approach. We groaned more loudly and looked with greater expectation. Our path was more direct. One day, Steve would lay his embattled body down and gather up a more beautiful garb. One day the eternal context would enfold our shabby temporal existence like a cloak. One day we would hold hands and explore the heights. But today, we shouldered our tent and slowly walked the narrow path, guided by our destination. Today, we drew strength from the center. We knew where we were going. I grasped his hand, and together, we took the next step.

40

MANNA

Saved Conference, Manila, 2012.

———◆———

Be strong and courageous.
Do not be frightened, and do not be dismayed,
for the Lord your God is with you wherever you go.

(Joshua 1:9)

Not long after our return to Manila, Steve had the opportunity to speak before a crowd of thousands in a packed stadium. After a video telling our story, he strode onto the stage to thunderous applause. The crowd was moved by the miraculous healing and they were praising God. I quietly prayed on the sidelines, knowing that his left leg was spasming and that he had struggled to climb the stairs to the stage without tripping.

Steve was indeed a miracle, but at the same time, we were still struggling in the desert. Sometimes the ongoing labor and toil of daily life obscured the miracle. Steve's movements were often stiff, his gait awkward, his wave an unnatural curve of fingers that could not bend or stretch, middle fingers always stuck at half-mast. His sensation remained obstinately absent, his nerves a confused tangle. The mundane, belabored tasks of moving—lifting boxes, shifting furniture—eluded him, so that he had to stand by helplessly and watch as I managed unpacking our new home. At other times, however, Steve accomplished some element of daily life so heroically—packing a suitcase, shepherding the children around a park, driving— that he seemed almost normal. Given how little he complained, one might forget that any suffering was going on at all. Casual observers had no indication of the effort it took for him to stand, much less to walk.

On the one hand, we heralded a miraculous amount of progress. It was easy to genuinely connect with joy when we considered the many hardships that we had been spared. On the other, we were frequently reminded that Steve's body remained significantly broken. A disconnect had developed between what the world saw and our actual experience. We were joyfully, miraculously well, and yet we remained among the walking wounded. We would sometimes forget that we were, in a sense, ill, and then suddenly we were reminded. Where previously Steve had hungered for new experiences, he now struggled with his appetite. The greater the experience, the greater the consequent drain on his physical stamina and resources. We took smaller bites. The thought of abandoning our tight partnership was painful, so I paced myself to his slow stride. In the process, however, my own appetite diminished. Some days I only wanted to hide myself away, my heart too tender to expose. It was not the disability itself that hurt the most, but the loss of a life fully lived.

We carried on. We yearned for the return of old patterns of life but repeatedly found that things could not be the same. As we reengaged with life, our limitations became more and more apparent. There was a danger of malaise. Someone who had been there asked, "So, have you hit a wall yet?" We were getting there. The progress had begun to slow. The weight of the reality of loss began to press in, even as Steve began to weary of the long march. The same person said that the second year was the hardest.

I thought of the Israelites, who did not have time to grumble when they were running for their lives from the Egyptians. But once they found themselves in the monotony of life in the desert, they began to complain. Even with enough sustenance for each day, the repetitive boredom wore on their ability to give thanks. Their eyes dimmed to the miracle of bread raining down from heaven.

I was like them, weary of the daily grind. The drama had subsided into a kind of discipline that sometimes dripped like water torture, an incessant, unchanging effort with few rewards that drained us of strength. We were entering that phase where the monotony of the regimen itself had become a hindrance. Sometimes we were tempted to give up. It was easy to lose sight of the greater rescue unfolding in our lives. We bought into the world-weary perspective of King Solomon and found nothing new in our days, tempting us to surrender our curiosity and hope. The landscape looked the same as it did last month and the month before that. There was no rain on the horizon, and the sun beat down on the desert floor.

The Bible is rife with stories of waiting. Moses and the Israelites wandered around the same patch of dry and inhospitable earth for forty years before reaching the Promised Land. Sarah waited ninety years to conceive. Jacob waited seven years to marry Rachel, working another seven to finish paying her bride-price. The book of Hebrews praises Abraham, Isaac, and Jacob, who waited until the end of their days and never saw the fulfillment of what was promised. In a four-day counseling intensive, the counselor said to Steve and me, "Of course, it will be ten years before you can make any sense out of this."

As I waited on God, I sensed equal parts comfort and exhortation. There are many comforting words in the Bible, many verses about love and compassion and rest. But there are other metaphors. Words like "battle" and "armor" are also used to describe our earthly passage. The verses that marked this section of road were not the ones I wanted to see as I stumbled toward the finish line. They said, "persist." They said, "keep going." They said, "do not give up." These were my sign posts:

Galatians 6:9. *Let us not become weary in doing good, for at the proper time we will reap a harvest if we do not give up.*

Romans 5:2-5. *And we boast in the hope of the glory of God. Not only so, but we also glory in our sufferings, because we know that suffering produces perseverance; perseverance, character; and character, hope. And hope does not put us to shame, because God's love has been poured out into our hearts through the Holy Spirit, who has been given to us.*

Habbakuk 3:17-19. *Though the fig tree does not bud and there are no grapes on the vines, though the olive crop fails and the fields produce no food, though there are no sheep in the pen and no cattle in the stalls, yet I will rejoice in the Lord, I will be joyful in God my Savior. The Sovereign Lord is my strength; he makes my feet like the feet of a deer, he enables me to tread on the heights.*

These scriptures were my manna. Daily I took them in. I put them on like gym clothes and stretched my spirit to their injunctions. Some days I felt impatient, not wanting to wait any longer. On those days, a verse from John 16:33 swam up into my spirit: "In this world, you will have trouble. But take heart! I have overcome the world." This is the long view. It is the faith perspective that stretches beyond what I can grasp into the leaping heart of hope. But while it pays to lift my eyes beyond the daily portion and gaze into that limitless expanse, some days I could not see. I could only reach down into the dryness of my spirit and offer up my dust and ashes, my rocks and even sometimes only my dirty, empty hands.

The Lord received my paltry offerings with tenderness. He reiterated His promises. He extended His mighty hand. But ultimately, what there was for me to do was steel my shoulders and keep pressing on. For the Israelites wandering in the desert, provision was measured in daily increments. Each morning the manna came. Whatever was kept beyond 24 hours rotted. Waking and sleeping are the natural brackets to what we can handle. Slow down, my soul. Endure this hour and the next. Run only this short distance.

At times, I cried out petulantly for rescue and relief. It would come, but in the meantime, there was work to be done. Each morning there was manna, whether I was grateful for it or not. Each day, I had enough, whether I was hungry or not. The key was to participate in the miracle. I could lie in my bed and grumble, or I could dust off hope and go out and gather my food. I determined to go out, anticipating the rescue. Though I was weary, I bent my knee to the ground to fill my arms with honeyed dew, for I could not escape the need to eat. Nor could I run from the One who is with me, a fiery pillar in the black of night. And when I thought I could go no further, I would find Him again, moving ahead of me, lighting the way.

EPILOGUE

*By entering through faith into what God has always wanted
to do for us—set us right with him, make us fit for him—we
have it all together with God because of our Master Jesus. And
that's not all: We throw open our doors to God and discover
at the same moment that he has already thrown open his door
to us. We find ourselves standing where we always hoped we
might stand—out in the wide open spaces of God's grace and
glory, standing tall and shouting our praise.*

There's more to come: We continue to shout our praise even when we're hemmed in with troubles, because we know how troubles can develop passionate patience in us, and how that patience in turn forges the tempered steel of virtue, keeping us alert for whatever God will do next. In alert expectancy such as this, we're never left feeling shortchanged. Quite the contrary—we can't round up enough containers to hold everything God generously pours into our lives through the Holy Spirit!

(Romans 5:2-5, The Message)

It has been six years now since the motorcycle accident that changed our lives. Steve's physical condition has remained much the same as described in the last chapter. He is a magnificent miracle living within the very real limitations of constant pain, strain, fatigue, weakness and loss of sensation. Our life together remains incredibly rich while also being deeply constrained and sometimes demanding. Together we live between a bold faith and belief that more healing is possible and a humble acceptance of what each day brings.

In these intervening years, I have swung back and forth between a confidence that God longs for healing for every believer and an understanding of the value of suffering for refinement, for instruction, for testing and for accomplishing God's purposes among us. I believe that both of these things are true. Healing has been achieved for all of us at a great price on the cross and we will possess that healing in glorious fullness for an eternity. In the meantime, we live in a real battleground waged with our free will, among the ruinous consequences of our own sin and alongside real evil that seeks to destroy. The fact is, none of us will be spared suffering, though we may taste the kingdom's goodness through signs and wonders at God's appointed times throughout our earthly lives. Those tastes are but dim reflections of what Christ has prepared for those who love Him, and yet they are delicious, fortifying us against the leaner periods that inevitably come.

It is the leaner years, however, that in retrospect seem to yield so much spiritual fruit. As Romans says, this is where our patience develops into real persistence and strength of character. Faith grows right in the middle of this very tension. To vacillate between these two polarities, God's healing power and the inevitability of suffering, is part of what it means to navigate the deeper mysteries of faith itself. I continue to find that the more I am able to cup my hands open in a posture of surrender, leaning into faith rather than the circumstances, the better I am able to hold both realities at the same time.

Perhaps the most surprising gift of the lean years that we have lived between the accident and the present is a growing sense of God's goodness irrespective of our circumstances. Amazingly, despite the fact that further healing has not come, the sweetness of a life lived with Jesus has only grown stronger on our lips and in our daily lives. Joy remains the dominant thread in the life of our family and in our marriage. While there are still moments of real despair when the pain feels too great and the mountain of a day seems too high to climb with Steve's weak limbs, there is nevertheless a greater understanding of the beautiful One who walks beside and the hope of glory toward which we walk together. How is this possible?

When we first encounter God's welcoming embrace, we are ushered into the wide open spaces of His grace and glory. We fall in love. When trouble inevitably comes and hems us in, we choose. This is the maturing part of faith, just as it is a maturing part of any marriage relationship. We either lean harder into His arms or run away from Him. If we choose to lean in, we receive the comfort of the Holy Spirit, the God of the Universe within us. In the deepest sense, we are not alone.

Leaning in does not mean that we no longer feel the pain. Rather, in the safety of His loving presence, the pain is freed to flow. The longer we walk together with God, the more easily these two things inhabit each other: the pain and His presence. His love becomes easier to find. We discover that its sphere stretches far beyond ourselves or even what we comprehend. The longer we live with faith, the wider love's circumference grows, beckoning us beyond ourselves and toward a greater world. I still ache to understand a love that envelops the entire universe, swallowing up time itself. It is this awesome breadth and width of love that holds our pain.

I am neither so pure nor so saintly as to perfectly align myself with love at all times. I do not always feel it, nor do I always bend toward its gentle instruction. But the bigger my understanding of His love gets, the smaller my inadequacies seem by comparison. Increasingly, I don't think He minds. He is perfectly patient with His perfect love, and generous to give it.

There is too much growth to call the place we now find

ourselves a desert. The trees are not yet tall, but there is adequate shade. The occasional bubbling spring delights. We are no longer thirsty on a daily basis, depending on miraculous provisions of water bursting forth from rocks. We are simply walking, together, wherever He leads.

We travelers, walking towards the sun, can't see
Ahead, but looking back the very light
That blinded us shows us the way we came,
Along which blessings now appear, risen
As if from sightlessness to sight, and we,
By blessings brightly lit, keep going toward
That blessed light that yet to us is dark.[3]

Wendell Berry

---

[3] Wendell Berry, "We travelers, walking to the sun," in *Given: New Poems* (Emeryville, Calif.: Shoemaker Hoard, an imprint of Avalon Publishing Group, Inc. 2005), p. 74.

MANY THANKS

———— ◆ ————

There are so many people to acknowledge in both the writing and the living of this book. I am convinced that Steve would not have recovered as he did without the prayers and the very real contributions of so many. There were those who brought meals, those who watched our children, those who contributed financially so that Steve could do therapy and so that our children could attend a wonderful school, those who put on fundraisers and those who built us a website. There were those who furnished our former home, worked in our garden, bought us furniture and put framed photos of our family all over the house so that we would feel at home. There were those who came and kneaded Steve's stiff fingers, and many therapists who provided their professional services for free. There were those who wrote often with words of encouragement and those who mobilized and organized our help. Some flew in from great distances and others helped clean out our flooded basement. Everyone, both friends and strangers alike, brought to us whatever they had in their hands to give, and each gift was a part of our healing. Thinking on this kindness still moves me to tears, and I will be forever grateful.

Thank you to those who helped with the writing of the book.

Thank you to Mandi Els, my earliest and most consistent cheer-leader. Thank you to my friends/editors who gave of their own private time to make this book better: Ron Carrucci, Dan and Becky Allender, Darlene Sala, Jennie Spohr, Sean Dimond, and Jennifer Chalmers. Thanks to Traci Mullins for whipping my thoughts into a more cohesive form. Thanks also to Zach Brittle for putting the final touches on this print edition of the book.

No one stood by us more than our family, who literally sheltered our children, picked us up, gave of their love, their time and their whole selves to help us stay afloat. We could not have done it without you. To John, Darlene, Rob, Richenda, Niclaa, Wim, David, Lena, Mark, Laura, Kim, Greg, Mike and Heather, we are eternally indebted and attached at the heart. Sean and Anne Dimond, you gave to us like family and you belong in this sacred circle as well. We cannot thank you enough.

To my husband Steve, whose steadfast love and kindness amazes me to this day, thank you for the gift of learning love together. You inspire me every day and I love you. To my children Aidan, Jude and Zephyr who were in themselves testaments of hope, thank you for being a reason to laugh and to find joy in the midst of every hardship.

This whole book is my love letter to God. Though I might have survived this trial without Him, I would not be the same. It is unlikely that my marriage, my family, and my hope would have survived without that greater grace. I am forever grateful to sail this ship of life with Someone greater than myself at its helm. No words suffice, and yet from the bottom of my heart I say, "Thank you!"

ABOUT THE AUTHOR

Michelle Ruetschle, © The Carrs Photography

Having grown up in seven countries across three continents, Michelle Ruetschle considers herself a true global nomad. Despite a brief and exciting career as an attorney, she finds her current endeavors raising three sons and being a pastor's wife in the Philippines equally enriching. Michelle loves books, film, photography and travel but finds her grandest adventures involve her lifelong discipleship journey with Jesus Christ. This is her first book.

FIND HER ORIGINAL BLOG AT STEVERUETSCHLE.COM.

Made in the USA
Middletown, DE
20 November 2018